# Multi-Engine

# Pilot

# Manual

JS314101C

# INTRODUCTION

The *Multi-Engine Pilot Manual* is a comprehensive textbook reference designed for private or commercial pilots who wish to add multi-engine ratings to their pilot certificates. It also will benefit rated multi-engine pilots who wish to update their skills with refresher training or to complete their biennial flight reviews.

The contents of the textbook apply to a wide range of light, twin-engine airplanes. Because of this, the emphasis is on general operational considerations and procedures. For specific information, multi-engine applicants should always refer to the pilot's operating handbook for their training aircraft.

The manual is divided into three parts: textbook information, exercises, and pilot briefings. The textbook section is divided into four chapters, which represent logical divisions of multi-engine training. Corresponding workbook exercises allow applicants to check their progress in the associated knowledge areas. At strategic points, pilot briefings may be used to provide the basis for in-depth discussions with an instructor, covering multi-engine operations, procedures, and maneuvers. The manual is supplemented with a comprehensive video cassette. Applicants who complete this program under the guidance of a qualified instructor will be well prepared for the FAA practical test.

# TABLE OF CONTENTS

# chapter 1

MULTI-ENGINE OPERATIONS AND SYSTEMS

## INTRODUCTION

The transition to the multi-engine airplane is exciting for most pilots, regardless of background experience. Suddenly they are exposed to an airplane with dramatically increased performance capabilities, compared to most single-engine airplanes. To derive the greatest benefit from multi-engine training, it is important that the applicant be familiar with the distinctive features of multi-engine flight.

The first section of this chapter provides the framework for transition to the multi-engine airplane under normal operating conditions. It introduces the concepts and considerations which are distinctive to multi-engine flight, such as aerodynamics, takeoff planning, flight profile, and maneuvers.

The second section of the chapter provides a comprehensive treatment of systems generally found on twin-engine airplanes. A broad knowledge of systems is an essential element of multi-engine training. The subjects covered in this chapter include propeller, fuel, fuel injection, electrical, landing gear, turbocharging, ice control, and cabin heating systems.

## SECTION A—PROCEDURES AND MANEUVERS

This section highlights the operational differences between multi-engine and single-engine airplanes. It begins with a discussion of twin-engine aerodynamics, defines important terms and concepts, and covers the preflight planning sequence. Following this is a description of a multi-engine flight profile and an analysis of typical maneuvers used during flight training, including a brief explanation of V-speeds.

Generally, this section is limited to normal two-engine operations; however, an understanding of many "single-engine" terms and concepts is required even for normal operations. Consequently, single-engine considerations are presented when necessary for clarification. For example, an understanding of the single-engine service ceiling and the accelerate-stop distance is necessary for normal takeoff planning.

# MULTI-ENGINE AERODYNAMICS

The principles of aerodynamics governing the flight of single-engine airplanes also apply to those with more than one engine. Multi-engine airplanes respond to the four forces of flight just as any other airplane, regardless of the number of powerplants. The primary aerodynamic differences between single-engine and multi-engine flight result from the location of the engines.

Figure 1-1 illustrates that thrust in conventional multi-engine airplanes is not directed along the centerline, as it is in airplanes with one engine. Conventional twin-engine airplanes have one engine mounted on each wing, producing thrust *parallel* to the longitudinal axis. Therefore, the thrust vectors are displaced from the airplane's centerline.

*Fig. 1-1. Thrust Comparison*

## INDUCED AIRFLOW

The most important advantage of wing-mounted engines is that a substantial amount of lift is derived from propeller slipstream. This *induced airflow* also occurs in single-engine airplanes; however, it is not as effective or apparent in aircraft where the powerplant is mounted along the centerline. Figure 1-2 illustrates the effect of induced airflow.

*Fig. 1-2. Induced Airflow*

The lift provided by induced flow is an important consideration during landing and in imminent stall recoveries. A sharp power reduction will cause an instantaneous loss of propeller slipstream flow and a corresponding loss of total lift. This could result in a high sink rate or stall if power is reduced suddenly during a slow final approach. On the other hand, rapid addition of power when an imminent stall has been identified could prevent further stall development. However, induced flow should never be relied on as the sole factor in stall recovery. The addition of power in combination with other normal stall recovery procedures should be utilized.

## TURNING TENDENCIES

In single-engine airplanes, left-turning tendencies are caused by both asymmetrical propeller loading (P-factor) and torque. Multi-engine airplanes have an even greater tendency to turn during climbs or other high angle of attack

Fig. 1-3. Asymmetrical Propeller Loading

maneuvers due to the additional engine and propeller. The position of these engines in relation to the airplane centerline causes asymmetrical propeller loading to exert a more forceful turning moment, as shown in figure 1-3. In addition, the effect of torque, which causes a rolling moment opposite the direction of propeller rotation, is also greater in multi-engine airplanes because of the more powerful engines. (See figure 1-4) In twins equipped with counterrotating engines, however, the effect of torque is eliminated. The

Fig. 1-4. Effect of Torque With Conventional Engines

torque from one engine cancels the effect of the other, as shown in figure 1-5. Similarly, the counterrotating engine configuration also eliminates the turning moment due to asymmetrical propeller loading.

Fig. 1-5. Effect of Torque With Counterrotating Engines

## MULTI-ENGINE CEILINGS

The maximum operating altitudes of airplanes in use today are as varied as the aircraft themselves. Some turbocharged light twins are designed to operate as high as 30,000 feet, while normally aspirated models are limited to altitudes between 15,000 and 20,000 feet under gross weight conditions.

Normally aspirated engines lose power progressively as the airplane ascends because of decreasing atmospheric pressure. This gradual loss of power determines the maximum altitude capabilities of the airplane. Contrary to popular belief, climb performance is based on excess power and not on the creation of additional lift. The amount of lift produced during a climb is nearly the same as the amount required for level flight.

Turbocharging increases the operating altitudes considerably over normally aspirated engines. It provides sea level or greater manifold pressure at high altitudes where normally aspirated engines can only provide manifold pressure equal to the ambient atmospheric pressure. However, there is a *critical altitude* where the atmosphere is too thin for the turbocharger to compress the air and maintain sea level manifold pressure. When climbing above this critical altitude, turbocharged engines progressively lose power like their normally aspirated counterparts.

### SERVICE CEILING

The *service ceiling* is defined as the maximum density altitude where the

*Fig. 1-6. Absolute Ceiling*

best rate-of-climb airspeed will produce a 100 f.p.m. climb at gross weight in the clean configuration with both engines producing maximum continuous power. The *single-engine* service ceiling refers to the altitude at which the rate of climb is 50 f.p.m. with one engine inoperative.

### ABSOLUTE CEILING

The *absolute ceiling* is defined as the maximum density altitude the airplane is capable of attaining or maintaining at gross weight, in the clean configuration, and at maximum continuous power. The absolute ceiling is closely related to the best angle-of-climb and best rate-of-climb speeds. Figure 1-6 shows that, as altitude increases, the best angle-of-climb speed increases, while the best rate-of-climb speed decreases. The point where the two speeds converge is the absolute ceiling of the airplane.

## MULTI-ENGINE V-SPEEDS

The chart in figure 1-7 lists the critical airspeeds (V-speeds) normally encountered in multi-engine flying. The pilot's operating handbook should be consulted for any additional airspeeds designated for a specific airplane. Practical applications of these airspeeds, including airplane performance planning and engine-out operations, are covered later in the text.

# PREFLIGHT PREPARATION

Multi-engine preflight activities include attention to normal details such as certificates and documents, weather, night flying techniques (if applicable), and aeromedical factors. In the area of flight planning, however, there are significant operational differences due to increased airplane performance and more complex performance calculations. These factors affect all phases of the planning process—takeoff and climb the most dramatically, and enroute and landing to a lesser degree. In addition, the pilot must also plan a course of action in the event of an engine failure.

## TAKEOFF AND CLIMB

Preflight planning begins with an accurate computation of density altitude. The pilot should compare density altitude with the *single-engine service ceiling* of the airplane. A combination of high airport elevation and high temperature often results in a density altitude above the single-engine service ceiling. Under these conditions, the probability of a sustained single-engine climb to a safe circling altitude is very remote. If an engine fails after liftoff, the only alternative may be a controlled descent to a forced landing.

Then, the pilot should analyze the airplane's runway requirement under existing conditions. This includes calculating both the takeoff roll and the *accelerate-stop distance*. This is the distance required to accelerate to a specified speed (usually liftoff speed) and, assuming an engine fails at exactly that speed, return to a full stop. The accelerate-stop distance under some conditions may be nearly *double* the normal takeoff roll, introducing a critical factor in preflight planning. For example, a pilot may determine that a 6,000-foot runway is adequate for a calculated takeoff roll of 3,400 feet. However, if the accelerate-stop distance for existing conditions is 6,500

| Designation | Description | Airplane Configuration or Significance of Speed | A/S Ind. Marking |
|---|---|---|---|
| $V_{SO}$ | Stalling Speed—Landing Configuration | Engines zero thrust, propellers takeoff position, landing gear extended, flaps in landing position, cowl flaps closed | Low speed end of white arc |
| $V_{S1}$ | Stalling Speed—Specified Configuration | Engines zero thrust, propellers takeoff position, landing gear and flaps retracted | Low speed end of green arc |
| $V_{MC}$* $V_{MCA}$ | Minimum Control Airspeed (Air Minimum Control Speed) | Takeoff or maximum available power on operating engine, critical engine windmilling (or feathered if auto feather device is installed), landing gear retracted, flaps in takeoff position, and CG at aft limit | Red radial line ** |
| $V_{SSE}$ | Intentional One Engine Inoperative Speed | Minimum speed for intentionally rendering one engine inoperative in flight for pilot training | |
| $V_X$ | Best Angle-of-Climb Speed | Speed which produces most altitude gain over a given distance with both engines operating; obstruction clearance speed | |
| $V_Y$ | Best Rate-of-Climb Speed | Speed which produces most altitude gain in a given time with both engines operating | |
| $V_{XSE}$ | Best Angle-of-Climb Speed (Single Engine) | Speed which produces most altitude gain over a given distance with one engine inoperative | |
| $V_{YSE}$ | Best Rate-of-Climb Speed (Single Engine) | Speed which produces most altitude gain in a given time with one engine inoperative | Blue radial line ** |
| $V_{LO}$ | Maximum Landing Gear Operating Speed | Maximum speed for safely extending or retracting the landing gear | |
| $V_{LE}$ | Maximum Landing Gear Extended Speed | Maximum speed for safe flight with landing gear extended | |
| $V_{FE}$ | Maximum Flap Extended Speed | Maximum speed with wing flaps in a prescribed extended position | High speed end of white arc |
| $V_A$ | Design Maneuvering Speed | Speed below which structural damage will not occur as a result of full control deflection | |
| $V_{NO}$ | Maximum Structural Cruising Speed | Maximum speed for normal operation | High speed end of green arc |
| $V_{NE}$ | Never-Exceed Speed | Maximum design speed without structural failure | Red line |

\* The FAA abbreviation $V_{MC}$ is used throughout this manual; however, some manufacturers may prefer $V_{MCA}$ in reference to this critical speed.

\*\* Aircraft receiving type certificates under FAR Part 23 after November 11, 1965

*Fig. 1-7.   Multi-Engine V-Speeds*

feet, the total safety of the takeoff is questionable. Therefore, the accelerate-stop distance is a primary limiting factor when evaluating airplane runway requirements.

The distance required to clear obstacles should include single-engine performance as well as twin-engine performance. The pilot must consider rising terrain and distant obstructions in conjunction with the anticipated single-engine rate of climb. When the density altitude and single-engine service ceiling are nearly the same, the terrain may rise more rapidly than the single-engine climb rate. In this situation, a single-engine climb to a safe circling altitude is unlikely.

Complete takeoff planning should involve a systematic evaluation of available alternatives. These can include suitable areas for a forced landing, nearby alternate airports, and the decision to takeoff with less fuel, baggage, and/or passengers. Finally, the pilot should review the engine-out airspeeds and procedures just prior to each takeoff. This makes each speed available for instant recall and is one of the final steps in pretakeoff planning.

Under normal climb conditions, a *cruise climb* is usually appropriate. This produces a slower rate of climb, but is advantageous since it decreases total trip time, allows better forward visibility, provides better engine cooling, increases passenger comfort, and may save fuel. However, if it is necessary to climb at a faster rate to reach favorable winds aloft or better weather, the best rate-of-climb airspeed ($V_Y$) can be used. Consult the pilot's operating handbook for performance charts to indicate the time, fuel, and distance required for climb to various altitudes.

An alternative would be the best angle-of-climb airspeed ($V_X$). This should be used only to clear obstructions im-

mediately after takeoff. A sustained climb at $V_X$ may result in an increase in the total trip time because of slower groundspeed. Long climbs at $V_X$ adversely affect engine cooling due to the high angle of attack and reduced airflow. Also, performance charts usually *are not* available for a sustained climb at $V_X$.

## ENROUTE

Enroute planning should include selection of the cruising altitude and an appropriate power setting. With this information, the airplane performance charts can be used to determine the true airspeed, range, and the enroute fuel consumption. The fuel consumption should be determined carefully to allow an adequate reserve in the event the flight cannot be completed as originally planned and diversion to an alternate airport is required.

Planning should also include consideration of the terrain, particularly in mountainous areas. This is especially important when the flight is conducted at altitudes above the single-engine service ceiling. In the event of engine failure, the pilot should plan a course of action for a gradual descent to the single-engine service ceiling. In this situation, it is important to know the location of lower terrain and alternate airports.

In summary, preflight planning for multi-engine operations must include several factors involving airplane performance. These performance areas and others, including landing, are covered in greater detail later in the text.

# MULTI-ENGINE OPERATIONS

## USE OF CHECKLISTS

Whether flying single- or multi-engine airplanes, the pilot should use printed checklists for each airplane. In some cases, checklists supplied by the manufacturer can be supplemented with minor additions for optional equipment installation. The most efficient way to use a checklist is to read each item aloud and actually touch or point to that item to ensure it is operating and/or positioned properly. When two pilots are available, a *command-response* checklist procedure is very effective. One pilot reads the checklist while the other pilot (usually the pilot in command) performs the required actions and acknowledges as each item is completed. Although command-response procedures apply mostly to airplanes requiring more than one crewmember, they can be useful in light twins whenever two pilots are available.

## VISUAL INSPECTION

A thorough preflight inspection is recommended prior to departure. The pilot's operating handbook should be consulted so important items are not overlooked. If the inspection reveals that the airplane has inoperative instruments or equipment, the pilot must determine if the inoperative items are essential for the safe operation of the intended flight. In the past, many operators and pilots have incorrectly used the listing in FAR Part 91.205 as the sole standard for determining whether or not their aircraft met the requirements for the operation being conducted. The rules now permit operation of certain general aviation aircraft with inoperative instruments and equipment within a framework of a controlled program of maintenance inspections, repairs, and parts replacements. These rules affect rotorcraft, nonturbine-powered airplanes, gliders, and lighter-than-air aircraft. The rules can be applied to single- or twin-engine aircraft with or without an approved Master Minimum Equipment List (MMEL). However, any person who has obtained an approved Minimum Equipment List (MEL) must continue to operate in accordance with its provisions. If that person elects to operate under the revised rules instead of following the MEL, then the MEL must

be surrendered to the FAA. All pilots should be familiar with FAR Parts 43.11, 91.213, and 91.405 which, among other provisions, require inoperative items to be placarded appropriately.

Inspection procedures during intermediate stops are normally limited to a check of the flight control hinges, fuel and oil quantity, and security of fuel and oil filler ports. However, if the airplane has been operated from marginal airports or in adverse weather conditions, a more extensive check should be performed. In addition, the pilot should inspect the airplane thoroughly after extended storage, when major maintenance has been performed, or after it has been exposed to extensive ground handling in crowded hangars.

When the preflight inspection is complete, the airplane is ready for boarding and the pilot must apply principles of good cockpit management. Cargo should be secured, seats adjusted and locked, seat belts and shoulder harnesses fastened, and the cabin door(s) secured. Equipment and materials necessary for the flight should be readily available. Passengers should be briefed on the use of seat belts, emergency procedures and equipment, and other pertinent items.

## STARTING ENGINES

Prior to starting any engine, the pilot should make a careful visual check of the area to ensure that it is clear and that the resulting propeller blast will not endanger people or property on the ramp. During engine starting at night, it may be advisable to turn the rotating beacon on momentarily to alert anyone in the area of the impending engine start. The position lights must be on for any night operations, including engine starts.

The airplane checklist usually contains starting procedures which are appropriate to the existing conditions. Normal, cold weather, hot start, and flooded engine procedures are provided. The checklist also may designate which engine is to be started first. In addition, the pilot should know the procedures for starting engines using external power. During the starting sequence, the pilot should monitor the engine instruments closely and check outside to ensure the airplane is not moving.

## TAXIING

During taxi, the pilot has three methods of directional control — the steerable nosewheel, differential braking, and differential power. For nearly all situations, nosewheel steering provides adequate maneuverability to taxi safely. However, if it is necessary to make tight turns at slow taxi speeds, differential power can be used. For example, to make a tight turn to the left, the power on the left engine is reduced and the power on the right engine is increased. At the same time, left rudder is applied. Figure 1-8 shows that the radius of turn depends on the amount of differential power applied. When using differential power, the pilot must exercise care to avoid creating a hazard to persons or property.

Prior to taxiing the airplane, the brakes should be checked for proper operation.

This check is most safely accomplished by applying a *small* amount of power to both engines to start the airplane moving, then reducing the power and applying the brakes. If any brake malfunction is noted, the airplane should not be taxied or flown until the problem is corrected. Safe taxi procedures also include consideration for wind and correct positioning of the flight controls to counteract its effect.

The least desirable method of directional control is differential braking. This technique increases the wear on both tires and brakes and can easily result in brake overheating and subsequent failure.

Increased directional control during crosswind taxiing can be accomplished by the use of differential power. As shown in figure 1-9, when additional power is applied to the upwind engine, a turning vector away from the wind is created. The velocity of the crosswind component determines the amount of differential that is required. However, if the crosswind velocity is quite high, the steerable nosewheel must be used to assist in directional control. Otherwise, high power on the upwind engine will result in excessive taxi speed and the need for frequent braking.

*Fig. 1-8. Differential Power for Turns*

THRUST COUNTERACTS TURNING TENDENCY

TURNING TENDENCY CAUSED BY WIND

WIND

*Fig. 1-9. Crosswind Taxi*

## PRETAKEOFF CHECK

Prior to takeoff, each airplane system is given a thorough functional check. Most of the items on the checklist are familiar to the pilot who has flown high performance single-engine airplanes, with the exception of the propeller feathering checks. Generally, multi-engine airplanes are equipped with full feathering propellers, which allow propeller rotation to be stopped in the event of an engine failure in flight. The check is performed by moving the propeller control lever to the full aft position and noting the change in engine r.p.m. If the propeller governor is operating properly, the r.p.m. should decrease rapidly as the propeller begins to feather. Then, the lever is moved full forward immediately to prevent the propeller blades from feathering. If the r.p.m. changes slowly or erratically, the feathering mechanism is not operating properly and in-flight feathering may not be possible. In this situation, flight should not be attempted before an authorized mechanic inspects and repairs the propeller system. An analysis of the propeller system is included in Section B of this chapter.

## NORMAL TAKEOFF

When the pretakeoff checklist is completed, the airplane is taxied onto the active runway and aligned carefully with the runway centerline. It is a good operating practice to bring the airplane to a complete stop on the runway prior to power application. As the power is advanced smoothly, the pilot should be alert for uneven thrust, signs of engine roughness, or sluggish engine acceleration. When takeoff power is attained, the engine instruments should be checked to determine that both engines are operating properly. This check should include the manifold pressure, r.p.m., fuel flow, and oil pressure/temperature. If any instrument indicates an abnormal system operation, the takeoff should be discontinued. The airspeed indicator also should be checked early in the takeoff run, since it is essential for safe flight in the event of engine failure.

During a normal takeoff, the airplane is allowed to accelerate to the recommended rotation and liftoff speed. Generally, this speed will be approximately $V_{MC}$ plus five knots. Under no conditions should the airplane become airborne at a speed less than the minimum single-engine control speed ($V_{MC}$). After liftoff, the airplane is accelerated to the two-engine best rate-of-climb airspeed ($V_Y$) and this speed is maintained until a safe maneuvering altitude is reached. $V_Y$ is used for this portion of the climb because it provides an adequate rate of climb and the speed normally is equal to or higher than the single-engine best rate-of-climb airspeed ($V_{YSE}$). Therefore, if an engine failure occurs, the airplane has already attained the airspeed which will produce the best single-engine climb performance.

Once the airplane is well clear of the runway, a positive rate of climb is established, and insufficient runway remains for landing, the landing gear should be retracted. It is recommended

SAFE MANEUVERING ALTITUDE

FIRST POWER
REDUCTION
CRUISE
CLIMB
                CLIMB AT $V_Y$

GEAR RETRACTION

$V_{MC}$ + 5 KNOTS

$V_{MC}$

ACCELERATE — STOP DISTANCE

ENGINE AND
INSTRUMENT CHECK

*Fig. 1-10.   Normal Takeoff and Climb*

that prior to retracting the landing gear, the brakes be applied momentarily to stop the rotation of the main wheels. Centrifugal force caused by the rapidly rotating wheels expands the diameter of the tires and, if ice or mud has accumulated in the wheelwells, the rotating wheels may rub as they enter.

The first power reduction should not take place until the landing gear is fully retracted and the airplane is at a safe maneuvering altitude. Once these two requirements are met, the power is reduced to the climb setting by decreasing the manifold pressure first, then the propeller r.p.m. When the climb power setting is established, the fuel pump for each engine is turned off *individually* and each mixture is adjusted for climb. The fuel pumps are not turned off simultaneously for safety reasons. Since an engine failure is more likely to occur during changes in power or fuel flow, one pump is turned off and the engine operation is monitored before the second pump is turned off. The same procedure is used when leaning the

mixtures or changing fuel tanks. The complete takeoff and climb profile is illustrated in figure 1-10.

### CROSSWIND TAKEOFF

Crosswind takeoffs in a multi-engine airplane require the same basic technique as that used in a single-engine airplane. Specifically, the upwind aileron is used to prevent side drift and rudder is used for directional control. As with other takeoffs, ground contact is maintained until the recommended liftoff speed is attained. Once the airplane is airborne, a crab is established to maintain the desired ground track. The landing gear is retracted when a positive rate of climb is established and a landing is no longer possible on the remaining runway.

## SHORT-FIELD TAKEOFF AND CLIMB

This maneuver may be divided into three separate phases — the takeoff ground run and liftoff, the first seg-

*Fig 1-11. Short-Field Takeoff and Climb*

ment of climb, and the second segment of climb. To begin the first phase of the maneuver, the airplane is taxied into position at the end of the runway, the flaps positioned at the recommended setting, the brakes applied, and full power applied to both engines. After the engines are developing full power, the brakes are released to begin the takeoff ground run.

As the airplane accelerates, the elevator control is maintained in the neutral position to create the least amount of aerodynamic drag. Then, elevator back pressure is applied to raise the nosewheel smoothly so the airplane breaks ground at $V_{MC}$ plus five knots or the recommended speed, whichever is greater. In no case should the airplane be allowed to lift off at a speed less than $V_{MC}$.

After the airplane breaks ground and a positive climb rate is established, $V_X$, or the recommended airspeed, whichever is greater, should be maintained until at least 50 feet AGL, or

until all obstacles are cleared. Then, the airplane should be accelerated to $V_Y$ for the second segment of the climb. Procedures for raising landing gear and flaps are found in the pilot's operating handbook. When a safe maneuvering altitude is reached, the power is reduced and a cruise climb established, if desired. Figure 1-11 illustrates the takeoff procedure and associated airspeed utilization.

## TAKEOFF CONSIDERATIONS

Every takeoff, regardless of the type, involves a very important consideration which results in safe multi-engine operations. Specifically, every takeoff must be planned and executed with the anticipation of an engine failure. If this habit pattern is established early in flight training and the situation does occur, the pilot will be prepared to perform the necessary procedures smoothly, accurately, and without hesitation.

## CLIMB

When a fast rate of climb is not required, passenger comfort should be considered.

Multi-engine airplanes generally have performance capabilities which produce a rate of climb in excess of 1,000 f.p.m. However, this high climb rate may result in considerable ear discomfort to the pilot and passengers. Therefore, an airspeed should be selected to produce a lower climb rate, such as 500 f.p.m. This technique results in added comfort, plus reduced trip time due to the higher airspeed used for climb.

When operating an airplane equipped with normally aspirated engines, climbs to high altitudes will require periodic increases in throttle settings to maintain a constant percent of power. Once the full throttle setting is reached, the percent of available horsepower will decrease, along with the aircraft's performance. When climbing at altitudes in excess of 5,000 feet MSL, the mixtures are leaned periodically to maintain smooth engine operation and maximum performance. If the airplane is turbocharged, 75 percent power normally is maintained throughout all or most of the climb. If 75 percent power is used, the mixture is adjusted to the climb fuel-flow setting until cruising altitude and power are established.

During climb operations, all of the engine instruments are monitored and maintained within the normal operating ranges. In particular, the cylinder head temperature is important due to the reduced airflow during the climb. The proper temperature range normally can be maintained by adjusting the cowl flaps (if appropriate). If cylinder head temperatures become excessive, the airplane may be leveled off momentarily or a higher climb speed may be selected. Additional procedures for combating high cylinder head temperatures include enriching the mixtures and increasing engine r.p.m.

### PROPELLER SYNCHRONIZATION

The propellers should be synchronized after the initial power reduction during the climb. If they are not rotating at the same r.p.m., an annoying, pulsating sound will be created within the cabin. As the difference in r.p.m. increases, the pulsation will increase. To synchronize the propellers, the pilot matches the r.p.m. indications on the tachometers, then slowly retards one propeller control and notes whether the sound increases or decreases. If the pulsation increases, the control lever is moved in the opposite direction until the pulsating sound stops. When the sound is eliminated, the propellers are synchronized.

## CRUISE

As the desired cruising altitude is reached, the airplane pitch attitude is reduced for level flight, the power setting adjusted, and the excess control pressures trimmed. After the airplane stabilizes in level flight, the mixture controls are adjusted to provide the best fuel-air ratio and, therefore, the best rate of fuel consumption for the power setting selected. The pilot's operating handbook should be consulted to determine the recommended fuel flow for the existing altitude and outside air temperature. Another method of adjusting the mixture is use of the exhaust gas temperature (EGT) gauge, which measures the temperature of the exhaust gases at the exhaust manifold. This method of adjusting the fuel-air mixture is the most accurate. The entire system is described in Section B of this chapter.

## DESCENT

The higher airspeeds and altitudes commonly used for flight in multi-engine airplanes generally require a planned descent profile for passenger comfort and satisfactory operation of such systems as turbocharging and cabin pressurization. Maintenance of normal engine temperatures also limits the rate of descent.

The following conditions can be used as an example of proper descent planning.

*Fig. 1-12. Stabilized Approach to Landing*

Cruising altitude .... 11,500 ft. MSL
Pattern altitude ....... 2,100 ft. MSL
Descent rate ............. 500 f.p.m.
Descent groundspeed ....... 155 kts.

The descent problem is solved by using the following steps.

1. Determine the required altitude loss of 9,400 feet by subtracting 2,100 feet from 11,500 feet.
2. Calculate the descent time by dividing 9,400 feet by 500 f.p.m., resulting in 18.8 minutes for the descent. (Round this to 19 minutes.)
3. Finally, use the flight computer to determine the distance required for the descent by finding the distance traveled in 19 minutes at a speed of 155 knots. This calculation indicates that 49 n.m. (57 s.m.) will be required. From these calculations, determine that a 500 f.p.m. descent should be initiated 49 n.m. from the destination to arrive at the airport at the proper altitude.

## LANDING

In a stabilized power approach, the power is established at a predetermined setting just prior to traffic pattern entry. The drag created by gear and flap extension slows the airplane to pattern airspeed and allows for the descent to landing with only minor power adjustments.

Figure 1-12 illustrates a typical traffic pattern used by most light and medium twin-engine airplanes. Although each make and model has slight procedural variances, the fundamentals of the traffic pattern and landing procedures are the same.

If the descent has been planned properly, the airplane should arrive at the traffic pattern altitude just before entering the downwind leg. Power is then adjusted to the desired setting. Once established on the downwind leg, the landing check is accomplished and the gear and flaps are extended according to the pilot's operating handbook. As the airplane decelerates, the recommended pattern speed should be established. When practical, this speed may be varied for other traffic in the pattern.

As the aircraft continues throughout the base leg and final approach, additional

*Fig. 1-13 Short-Field Approach and Landing*

flaps are extended to control the airspeed and descent rate. On final approach the pilot should verify that the propeller controls are positioned at high r.p.m. and the mixtures are set for the appropriate altitude. Ideally, the power is reduced gradually as the airplane approaches touchdown in the proper landing attitude. After touchdown, directional control is maintained through the combined use of rudder and nosewheel steering. The brakes are used, as necessary, to slow the aircraft and the flaps may be raised to increase braking efficiency.

Crosswind landings are made using either the crab method, the wing-low method, or a combination of the two. Any crab used is removed with downwind rudder just prior to touchdown in a near three-point attitude. When landing in strong crosswinds, the minimum flaps necessary for the runway length are used.

## SHORT-FIELD APPROACH AND LANDING

This approach and landing procedure involves maneuvering the airplane over a 50-foot obstacle to a landing using the shortest possible roll-out distance. The approach and landing are per-

formed with full flaps to achieve a slower approach speed and steeper descent angle.

The downwind and base leg portions of the short-field landing traffic pattern are the same as those used for a normal landing. The difference between the two procedures is found on the final approach in that a slightly higher approach is planned to clear the obstacle. The final approach is planned so that full flaps are extended, a constant airspeed is established, and a constant angle of descent is used throughout the approach. The power should remain nearly constant until the landing flare, where the throttles are closed smoothly so touchdown can be made within 100 feet of the landing point with little or no floating. After landing, elevator back pressure is maintained, braking is applied as necessary, and flaps are retracted as recommended. Figure 1-13 illustrates the short-field approach and landing technique.

## GO-AROUND

For a two-engine go-around from a rejected (balked) landing, the pilot normally applies full throttle, since the propeller and mixture controls were positioned on final for a possible go-around. The next step is to reduce drag as much as possible and initiate a climb at the recommended airspeed. Flaps and landing gear are retracted in the sequence specified in the pilot's operating handbook. This may require the flaps to be set immediately to the takeoff setting. Since the power application and flap retraction may cause a large trim change, the pilot should trim the aircraft, as necessary. After all obstacles are cleared, any remaining flaps are retracted and the recommended climb speed (usually $V_Y$) is established. After the airplane is established in the new configuration and a safe altitude is reached, power is reduced and appropriate checklists are completed.

# MULTI-ENGINE FLIGHT MANEUVERS

Since multi-engine practical test standards include several maneuvers flown at speeds near the actual stalling speed, recovery or completion must be accomplished no lower than 3,000 feet AGL. These maneuvers include steep power turns, stalls, and maneuvering during slow flight.

## STEEP TURNS

Steep turns for a commercial pilot certificate are performed with a bank angle of 50°, ±5°. These turns should not be performed at speeds in excess of maneuvering speed due to the high load factors that may be induced.

Small pitch changes will result in greater altitude variations because of the higher airspeeds involved and the greater amount of excess power available. Therefore, special attention is necessary for smooth and coordinated control usage, including trim. Each of the flight instruments is monitored for precise references, and outside visual cues are checked for any indication of a deviation from the proper pitch attitude. Corrections are made promptly before any large correction is needed to maintain the desired altitude and bank angle. Steep turns are

done at a constant airspeed and altitude. The pilot completes a 360° turn immediately followed by at least a 360° turn in the opposite direction. The pilot exits the maneuver by rolling out on the original entry heading.

## MANEUVERING DURING SLOW FLIGHT

Slow flight is conducted with both engines operating and at an airspeed sufficiently slow that any further increase in angle of attack or load factor will result in a stall. This is accomplished in both cruise and landing configurations. The maneuver can be performed during straight and level or during turns.

To enter the maneuver, the power is reduced to approximately 12 to 15 inches of manifold pressure and the attitude is increased slowly as the airspeed decreases. Approximately five knots above the desired airspeed, the power is increased to stop the deceleration. If the maneuver is performed in the landing configuration, the gear and flaps are extended at the appropriate airspeeds as the airplane decelerates. Considerably more power is required to maintain altitude in the landing configuration because of the large amount of drag. Several transitions between the cruise and landing configuration should be practiced so the maneuver can be performed at a constant altitude and heading.

To return to level flight the flaps are reduced to the takeoff position, the landing gear is retracted, and the remaining flaps are retracted as the speed increases. Throughout the transition and during the maneuver, the airplane heading and altitude must remain constant.

## STALLS

The applicant for a multi-engine class rating is required to demonstrate stall recognition and recovery. Stalls are performed with and without power, in straight and level and turning flight, and

*Fig. 1-14. Power-Off Stall—Approach-to-Landing Configuration*

with various gear and flap configurations. On no occasion is the pilot required to demonstrate a stall with any engine throttled and the other engine developing effective power. Performance of a stall in an aircraft which is producing asymmetrical power can cause a spin or other dangerous situation.

During a multi-engine practical test, the applicant must demonstrate power-on and power-off stalls. Generally, recovery is initiated at the first aerodynamic indication of a stall (buffeting or decay of control effectiveness) unless the pilot's operating handbook specifies recovery prompted by an artificial warning system, such as a stall warning horn. The pilot should avoid excessive pitch changes and secondary stalls, and be able to recover to a specific airspeed and configuration.

### POWER-OFF STALLS

Before practicing power-off stalls, the area is checked for other traffic and power is adjusted as necessary. Gear and flaps are extended, and the airspeed is stabilized at $V_{YSE}$. If desired, a level turn may be initiated. Power is then

reduced and the pitch attitude is increased to slow the airplane. A gradual pitch increase that reduces the airspeed by approximately one knot per second prevents an excessive altitude gain.

As the airplane decelerates, there are three basic indications of an approaching stall — reduction in sound level, decreasing control effectiveness, and aerodynamic buffeting. The reduction in the tone and intensity of slipstream noise and the change in engine sounds are useful indications of an approaching stall. As the controls become progressively less responsive, a point will be reached where a slight aerodynamic buffet is felt.

As soon as this buffet begins, recovery should be initiated. It is important to use the proper recovery sequence to break the stall and reduce drag so the airplane will accelerate as quickly as possible. There are three steps in this sequence, as shown in figure 1-14.

1. Reduce angle of attack and apply full power while leveling the wings.
2. Raise flaps to the takeoff setting.
3. Retract the landing gear after a positive rate of climb is established.

## POWER-ON STALLS

This maneuver simulates a steep climb, since this type of stall is most likely to occur during a climb over an obstacle. The power-on stall maneuver should normally be done at less than full power to avoid a high pitch attitude and excessive altitude gain as airspeed decreases. The gear is normally retracted; however, flaps may or may not be extended depending on the situation being simulated. First, the area is checked for other traffic and the desired airspeed is established, then pitch attitude is increased to approach the stall. As with the approach and landing stall, the pitch change should be gradual to prevent the airplane from attaining an abnormal nose-high pitch attitude.

As this attitude is maintained, the decreasing sound level and reduced control response give progressive indications of the approaching stall. At the first aerodynamic indication of a stall (as the buffeting begins), the nose is lowered smoothly and full power applied. The aircraft is then allowed to accelerate to best angle-of-climb speed and the climb is resumed.

## ACCELERATED MANEUVER STALLS

Multi-engine applicants do not practice accelerated maneuver stalls. They are not among the required tasks on flight tests. However, all pilots should be aware of the flight parameters and characteristics of this type of stall. The term "accelerated" is not related to the rapidity of stall onset. Instead, it refers to a stall which occurs at a higher-than-normal airspeed because of an increased load factor. Normally, a steep turn is the maneuver most likely to cause an accelerated stall.

During this type of stall, the decreasing sound level and progressively sluggish control response associated with other stalls do not occur to the same degree. This is due to the fact that the aircraft stalls at a higher speed. Therefore, the major aerodynamic indication of the accelerated stall is buffeting. When this occurs, recovery should be initiated immediately. Multi-engine pilots should avoid demonstrations of accelerated maneuver stalls, since repeated practice may cause structural damage to the airplane. Also, this type of maneuver should never be performed in any airplane which is prohibited from such maneuvers by its type-certificate restrictions.

## STALL/SPIN AWARENESS

While stall/spin awareness has always been an important part of pilot training, regulatory changes to FAR Part 61 and Part 141 now require additional ground and flight training in this area. These regulations affect both aeronautical knowledge and flight proficiency requirements for recreational, private, and commercial pilot applicants who are seeking airplane or glider category ratings. For the practical test, applicants must be able to explain the aerodynamic factors of a spin including instrument indications, phases of a spin (with regard to uncoordinated flight), vertical and rotational velocities, and the rotation about the axis perpendicular to the earth's surface. In addition, applicants must explain situations where unintentional spins may occur, as well as the technique used to recognize and recover from unintentional spins. Refer to *Stall and Spin Awareness Training* (AC 61-67 as amended).

## EMERGENCY DESCENT

Most POHs include emergency descent procedures for incidents such as an in-flight fire, or sudden loss of pressurization. The instructor should emphasize the importance of following the emergency descent procedure listed in the POH for the specific emergency. Emergency descent considerations may include high drag configurations (gear and flaps down), the use of carburetor heat, and observing specific V-speed and aircraft structural limitations. An emergency descent may involve fairly high airspeeds and positive G loading.

# SECTION B—GENERAL SYSTEMS

The following section provides the multi-engine applicant with a general overview of representative systems incorporated on modern twin-engine airplanes. This section is *not* designed to be used in lieu of the specific pilot's operating handbook, but, rather, to acquaint the pilot with the major systems and system variations found in general aviation airplanes. *For specific operational details and limitations, the appropriate pilot's operating handbook must be consulted.*

## PROPELLER SYSTEMS

The propellers installed on most multi-engine aircraft may be classified as constant speed, controllable pitch, full feathering propellers. Depending on the propeller manufacturer, there are two types of controlling mechanisms. The first utilizes boosted engine oil pressure and nitrogen pressure within the propeller hub. The second system uses boosted engine oil pressure and mechanical springs for system operation.

### CONSTANT SPEED PROPELLERS

When a fixed pitch propeller system is installed on an aircraft, the propeller r.p.m. changes according to the speed and angle of attack of the airplane. For example, if the airplane begins to accelerate, the propeller r.p.m. tends to increase. Conversely, if the airspeed decreases, as in a climb, the propeller r.p.m. decreases. The constant speed system eliminates propeller r.p.m. fluctuation by changing the *blade angle* automatically according to the conditions. If the airspeed increases, the blade angle increases; conversely, when the airplane decelerates, the blade angle decreases automatically. Maintenance of a constant r.p.m. by variation of the propeller blade angle also tends to maintain the desired propeller angle of attack and optimum propeller efficiency. The constant speed system requires a hydraulic propeller governor and pitch change mechanism.

When the propeller control lever is adjusted to the desired r.p.m., the hydraulic governor is thereby adjusted to maintain that r.p.m. If the engine speed begins to increase above the r.p.m. for which the governor is adjusted, the governor actuates the pitch-change mechanism in the propeller hub and the blade angle increases. When the blade angle increases, the angle of attack is increased, resulting in higher drag loading. The increased load causes a lower propeller speed. As the engine r.p.m. decreases, the governor reverses the process in the pitch-change mechanism, which returns the blade angle to the original pitch and the engine to the desired speed. When the engine speed begins to decrease below the selected r.p.m., the process is the same, except the blade angle is decreased.

### PROPELLER CONTROLS

The propeller control levers allow the pilot to select the desired r.p.m., which the constant speed system will then maintain. To select the desired setting, the controls are moved either forward or aft. If the controls are moved full forward, the blade angle is decreased and high r.p.m. results. When the controls are moved aft, the governor increases the blade angle and the r.p.m. decreases. If the propeller control levers are moved to the full aft position into the feather detents, the blade angle is increased to nearly align with the relative wind. This action stops the rotation of the propeller, as shown in figure 1-15.

*Fig. 1-15. Propeller in Full Feather*

The purpose of the full feathering propeller is to eliminate the parasite drag developed by a windmilling propeller. When the propeller is windmilling, the drag is increased greatly and airplane performance is decreased significantly. This consideration becomes critical during engine-out operations.

## FEATHERING

Since the propellers on multi-engine airplanes are not only constant speed but also full feathering, two mechanisms are required to change the blade angle from low pitch to full feather. The basic pitch-change mechanism depends on boosted engine oil pressure from the propeller governors. However, if the pitch-change mechanism depended entirely on oil pressure to feather the propeller, the loss of oil pressure or governor failure would prevent the propeller from being feathered. Therefore, a secondary method of increasing blade angle is required for full feathering pitch-change mechanisms.

When the propeller is spinning, the normal aerodynamic twisting forces are acting on the propeller to move it towards low pitch (high r.p.m.). These forces can be altered by changing the blade's center of mass in lieu of opposing oil pressure from the propeller governor. To alter the center of mass, featherable propellers have counterweights attached to the base of each blade, as shown in figure 1-16. As the propeller rotates, the counterweight's center of mass moves toward the blade's plane of rotation, tending to increase the blade angle, as shown in figure 1-17. The centrifugal force produced by the counterweights is designed to be slightly *greater* than the aerodynamic twisting force, and hydraulic pressure is used to aid the aerodynamic force in decreasing the blade angle. In addition to the counterweights, the propeller system incorporates either compressed air or a mechanical spring to aid in moving the blades to the full feather position.

*Fig. 1-16. Propeller Counterweights*

An important aspect of the feathering procedure is engine speed. A locking device in the propeller hub prevents feathering the propeller at lower engine speeds, usually below 700 to 800 r.p.m. This insures that the propeller does not feather during engine starting or shutdown, when the engine oil pressure is very low. The pilot's operating handbook should be consulted for specific operational details.

## POWER APPLICATION OR REDUCTION

Correct propeller operation is directly related to proper engine care. In flight, it is very important to maintain the manifold pressure and propeller r.p.m. within their respective operating ranges. For specific limitations and guidelines, the appropriate pilot's operating handbook should be consulted.

Proper propeller operation is critical during the phases of flight requiring power application or reduction. Because the propellers are constant speed, the basic operating procedures must be followed. Specifically, for power application, the propeller control levers must be advanced first, followed by increases in manifold pressure. For power reduction, the manifold pressure must be reduced prior to reduction in propeller r.p.m. This procedure maintains the proper balance between internal cylinder pressure and the power required of the engine.

*Fig. 1-17. Effect of Counterweights*

## PROPELLER SYNCHRONIZING SYSTEM

Propeller synchronizing systems are installed on some multi-engine airplanes to match the r.p.m. of the two engines automatically. The system operates on the principle that one engine is slaved to the other. For example, the left engine follows any change in r.p.m. of the right engine. This type of system aids in elimination of propeller vibration and noise within the cabin.

System operation is simple in that the pilot first sets the desired r.p.m. of both propellers, insuring that the two propellers are within 50 r.p.m. of each other. When the propeller synchronizer switch is activated, the propeller r.p.m. of the left engine will follow changes in r.p.m. of the right engine over a *limited range* of engine speeds. This limited range prevents the left engine from losing more than 50 propeller r.p.m. in the event the right engine is feathered with the synchronizer system activated. The limitation placed upon the use of the system is that it must be deenergized during takeoffs, landings, and single-engine operation.

## AUTOFEATHER SYSTEM

Autofeather systems are installed on some high performance turboprop twin-engine airplanes to feather the propeller automatically in the event of a power loss during takeoff. The system is armed for operation prior to takeoff and turned off during the climb when a safe altitude is reached.

The autofeather system is an electrically energized system using microswitches in the power levers and a power sensing switch within the engine system. As the power levers are advanced for takeoff, the microswitches are activated and the system is *armed* for operation. In the event either engine loses power during the takeoff ground run, rotation, or early phases of climb, the power sensing switch senses the power loss. At that time, the autofeather system causes a drop in oil pressure from the propeller governor and the propeller on the failed engine feathers automatically. Once the propeller has been feathered by the autofeather system, the pilot must be cautious *not* to retard the power lever on the failed engine until the system has been deenergized. If the power lever is retarded, the microswitch is opened.

*Fig. 1-18. Blade Angle Range*

This deactivates the system and the propeller may unfeather. Therefore, when a propeller feathers, the autofeather should be deenergized and normal engine shutdown procedures followed.

## REVERSIBLE PROPELLER SYSTEM

As an additional system feature of turboprop powered twin-engine airplanes, reversible propellers are installed to decrease the landing roll. A reversible propeller does not reverse in direction of rotation, but merely changes blade angle into the *negative* blade angle range. For example, the *total range* of a particular propeller may be +87° to -19° blade angle. The blade angle for feather would be +87°, while the cruise blade angle may be +11° to +17°. The taxi blade angle may be +9°, zero thrust may be +2° and the reverse range may be 0° to -19°. This concept is shown in figure 1-18.

The propeller that has reversing capability simply uses a negative blade angle in conjunction with engine power to create reverse thrust. The negative blade angle is created by increasing the oil pressure in the propeller hub to force the blades to a negative angle of attack. The in-crease in oil pressure occurs when the power levers are moved into the reverse range, which signals the propeller governor to increase oil pressure. Each power lever controls its respective engine and reversing capability.

## FUEL SYSTEMS

The fuel systems installed on most general aviation multi-engine airplanes are designed for simplicity and ease of operation. Although each individual airplane system may have operational and structural differences, all fuel systems have the same basic components.

The fuel system may be described as two independent systems, one installed in each wing, which permit each engine to operate from its own fuel supply. The two systems are interconnected by crossfeed lines which allow the distribution of fuel from one tank to the opposite engine, if necessary. The following paragraphs present a discussion of common fuel system components.

### SYSTEM COMPONENTS

#### FUEL TANKS

The fuel cells, or fuel tanks, generally are located within each wing, outboard of

*Fig. 1-19. Interconnected Fuel Tank Installation*

the engine. Some models of airplanes utilize a multi-tank installation where as many as four tanks are incorporated internally within each wing. These tanks generally have one filler port and are interconnected to provide a single source of fuel for the respective engine. This installation is shown in figure 1-19.

Some types of airplanes, however, utilize individual tank installations which are designated as the *main tank* and *auxiliary tank*. These fuel tanks may be installed internally at different locations within the wing or externally on the wingtips. Generally, they have individual filler ports and are not interconnected. Therefore, each tank provides an individual fuel supply to the engines, as shown in figure 1-20.

## FUEL PUMPS

The fuel system of any multi-engine airplane incorporates two types of pumps to provide fuel pressure to the engine. The first type is a mechanical engine-driven pump installed on each engine. The second type is an electric boost pump which is operated by a simple switch located on the control panel. There are two electric pumps (one for each engine) installed within the fuel system. Their locations vary between makes and models of airplanes.

### Engine-Driven Fuel Pumps

One engine-driven fuel pump is installed on each engine upstream from the fuel injection unit. The pump draws fuel

*Fig. 1-20. Main/Auxiliary Fuel Tanks*

from the tanks and forces it through the injector unit. Since this type of pump is mechanically actuated, it is dependent upon operation of the engine. Therefore, during the engine start procedure, the electric boost pump must be activated to provide fuel to the engine. After the engine is running smoothly, the electric pump is turned off and the mechanical pump should provide adequate fuel pressure.

### Electric Fuel Pumps

Electric fuel pumps are installed for two purposes—to provide fuel pressure during engine start and to provide fuel pressure in the event a mechanical pump should fail or malfunction. Therefore, most systems require the electric pump to be in operation during periods when an engine-driven pump failure could be critical. Such situations include takeoffs, landings, and maneuvering at slow airspeeds and/or low altitudes.

The locations of the electric pumps within the fuel system vary according to the airplane manufacturer, but two basic locations are typically used. The first type is installed within the engine nacelle upstream from the mechanical pump. The second type is located within each main fuel tank, submerged in the fuel. Although these pumps are located in different positions within the system, both are capable of providing adequate fuel pressure to sustain nearly maximum engine power in the event of a mechanical pump failure.

### Operational Check

The engine starting procedure provides a check of both the electric pump and the mechanical pump for proper operation. During the engine start, the electric pump should provide fuel flow and pressure with the fuel selector on and the mixture control full rich.

The engine-driven mechanical pump may be checked by simply turning off the electric pump after the engine is running smoothly. If the mechanical pump is inoperative, the engine will fail due to insufficient fuel pressure. The combination of the two pumps is critical to safety, and flight must not be attempted when either pump is malfunctioning.

### FUEL SELECTOR CONTROL

The fuel selector controls are located inside the cabin and may vary in appearance and operation, depending on the airplane manufacturer. The fuel selector control shown in figure 1-21 is a three-position selector which allows the pilot to select either on, off, or crossfeed for each engine. With this type of system, fuel can be transferred from one side of the airplane to the engine on the opposite side. Therefore, all of the fuel is considered to be available for crossfeed operations.

*Fig. 1-21. Three-Position Fuel Selector Control*

Figure 1-22 depicts another type of common fuel selector control. Each control has four positions, indicating main, auxiliary, crossfeed, and off. This type of fuel selector control is utilized on airplanes that have auxiliary fuel tanks not interconnected with the main tanks. When the auxiliary tanks are selected, no fuel is used from the main tanks.

*Fig. 1-22. Four-Position Fuel Selector Control*

### FUEL SELECTOR VALVES

Fuel selector valves have the function of routing the fuel from the appropriate tank to the engine. These valves generally are operated through a mechanical linkage from the fuel selector control inside the airplane. All fuel must pass through the fuel selector valves enroute from the tank to the engine. In the event a fuel selector valve is malfunctioning, the fuel selector control will not seat properly in the detents or the control will be difficult to move. If either of these difficulties occur, a mechanic should be consulted prior to starting the engines.

### CROSSFEED SYSTEM

The crossfeed feature of any fuel system allows the pilot to direct fuel from one side of the airplane to the opposite engine. However, the individual pilot's operating handbook should be consulted for specific crossfeed system operation and limitations. The fuel from all tanks may not be available for crossfeed purposes.

Generally, the crossfeed system is utilized during emergency single-engine operations. For example, if the right engine is inoperative, the crossfeed may be used to direct fuel from the right tanks to the left engine. If extended single-engine flight becomes necessary, fuel usage from each side of the airplane should be alternated approximately every 30 minutes. In this manner, fuel will be consumed so it equalizes the weight distribution between the two sides of the airplane.

## FUEL TANK VENTS

Although the fuel tank vents are a small portion of the total fuel system, they are vital to its proper operation. These vents may be located in a variety of positions, but all serve the purpose of allowing air to replace the fuel that is consumed by the engines. In addition, some types of fuel vents are exposed to ram air pressure, which creates a downward pressure on the fuel within the tank. This slight additional pressure aids the fuel pumps in delivering fuel to the engines.

In the event a fuel tank vent is blocked, a vacuum is created within the tank as the engine consumes the fuel. This condition results in engine failure due to fuel starvation. Therefore, the fuel tank vents are an important preflight inspection item and should be checked for blockage due to wax, dirt, or other foreign material. As an additional precaution, it may be recommended that extremely dusty conditions be avoided during taxi and takeoff.

## FUEL STRAINERS

The fuel strainers (sometimes termed gascolators) are installed to filter and trap any accumulations of moisture or sediment in the fuel supply. One strainer is installed on each engine between the fuel selector valve and the engine-driven fuel pump. As the fuel passes through the strainer enroute to the fuel pump, the water and/or debris accumulates in the bottom of the strainer bowl, as

Fig. 1-23. Fuel Strainer

shown in figure 1-23. During the preflight inspection, the quick drain is opened momentarily to remove the accumulation of contaminants.

## QUICK DRAINS

In addition to the quick drains located on the fuel strainers, quick drains are usually installed for each fuel tank and crossfeed line. Each drain should be opened momentarily during the preflight inspection to remove any contaminants that have settled to the bottom of the tank or fuel line. The opening of the fuel tank and fuel line quick drains should be accomplished *prior* to draining the strainers. If the strainer is drained before the fuel tanks, a portion of the fuel within the tank is moved towards the strainer. This movement disturbs the fuel and the contaminants within the tank and makes removal of the contaminants virtually impossible until they have settled back to the bottom of the tank. Therefore, the pilot should drain the outboard tank first, followed by the inboard tank, then the strainer, and finally the crossfeed lines.

## FUEL SYSTEM MONITORING INSTRUMENTS

The instruments associated with most fuel systems are the fuel-pressure and fuel-flow gauges, as shown in figure 1-24.

*Fig. 1-24. Fuel System Monitoring Instruments*

The indications of these instruments should be monitored during the entire flight.

### Fuel-Pressure Gauge

The fuel-pressure gauge indicates fuel pressure at the injector inlet. The gauge is marked with a green arc to indicate the normal range of fuel pressure. In addition to the pressure gauge, some types of airplanes are equipped with warning lights to alert the pilot to low fuel pressure. If inadequate pressure is observed or the warning lights illuminate, the electric fuel pump should be activated, since the mechanical pump may be malfunctioning. The following list describes several conditions which can create low fuel pressure.

1. Damaged fuel selector valve
2. Fuel selector control in improper position
3. Blocked or broken fuel line
4. Blocked fuel tank vent
5. Malfunctioning fuel pump

### Fuel-Flow Gauge

The fuel-flow gauge indicates fuel consumption of each engine measured in gallons and/or pounds per hour. The instrument measures fuel flow by sensing a pressure drop within the fuel-flow divider. When a constant pressure is supplied to the engine-driven fuel pump, the pressure downstream may be mea-

sured against the constant static pressure. The constant static pressure is available through a vent line extending from the gauge to the engine compartment, which automatically compensates the instrument for altitude. When the instrument measures the two pressures, the resultant differential pressure can be calibrated in gallons or pounds per hour of fuel flow.

# FUEL INJECTION SYSTEM

Control of fuel and air entering the combustion chamber is one of the most critical factors in operating high performance engines. Extremes in fuel-air mixtures, pressures, and temperatures can greatly reduce an engine's performance, or even cause it to fail. Although float carburetion may be an adequate means of control in some cases, fuel injection provides a more accurate method of measuring and distributing the desired amount of fuel to each cylinder. The contribution of fuel injection to an engine's overall performance can be shown in terms of lower fuel consumption per unit of horsepower, increased horsepower per unit of engine weight, and lower operating temperatures.

## SYSTEM COMPONENTS

Fuel injection systems are utilized on most modern multi-engine airplanes. Since each individual airplane may have slightly different operating procedures and characteristics, a careful review of the appropriate pilot's operating handbook is required prior to operating an unfamiliar system.

As shown in figure 1-25, the continuous flow fuel injection system has four basic components. The numbered callouts in the illustration correspond to the following items.

1. Engine-driven fuel pump
2. Fuel injector unit
3. Fuel-flow divider
4. Individual fuel injection nozzles

AIR INTAKE MANIFOLD
DIRECTS AIR TO
CYLINDERS

CHECK
VALVE

ELECTRIC
ROTARY-TYPE
FUEL PUMP

RAM AIR

| AIR FLOW | | FUEL FLOW | |
|---|---|---|---|
| | RAM | | UNPRESSURIZED |
| | THROTTLED | | PRESSURIZED |
| | | | METERED |

*Fig. 1-25. Fuel Injection System Components*

Fuel is delivered from the airplane's tanks to the engine-driven fuel pump, where the fuel is put under pressure. The pressurized fuel is routed through the fuel injector unit, where the fuel flow is metered by a set of valves according to the mixture setting and flow of air to the engine. Also, the intake airflow is throttled in the fuel injector unit. The metered fuel then is sent to the fuel-flow divider, where it is divided equally among the individual fuel lines that lead to each cylinder. The fuel lines carry the metered and divided fuel to the individual discharge nozzles where the fuel is atomized, then vaporized at the cylinder's intake port.

## ENGINE-DRIVEN FUEL PUMP

The engine-driven fuel pump is the only constantly moving part in the continuous flow fuel injection system. This fuel pump is attached to the engine's accessory drive section. An electric fuel pump also is incorporated to provide fuel pressure for engine starting and to deal with possible failure of the engine-driven pump.

## FUEL INJECTOR UNIT

The function of the fuel injector unit is similar to that of the carburetor in a conventional fuel-air induction system. The difference is that the fuel and air are

FLAME FRONT ADVANCING SMOOTHLY, UNDER CONTROL

*Fig. 1-26. Normal Combustion Process*

not combined in the fuel injector unit. Instead, this unit regulates the air flowing through the air induction manifold and meters the correct amount of fuel required for the fuel injectors.

### FUEL-FLOW DIVIDER

The fuel-flow divider, sometimes termed the fuel manifold, is designed to divide the fuel evenly between each of the cylinders. Valves are built into the flow divider to provide a positive fuel shutoff mechanism when the mixture control is moved to idle cutoff.

### FUEL INJECTION NOZZLES

The fuel nozzles inject the metered fuel into the air induction manifold. Injection actually occurs in the cylinder head, just outside the intake valves and ports leading to the combustion chambers. The fuel is mixed with the intake air just before entering the combustion chamber.

### FUEL-FLOW INDICATOR

A fuel-flow indicator enables the pilot to monitor the operation of the system, as well as determine the extent to which the mixture may be leaned. The fuel-flow indicator is actually a pressure gauge connected to the fuel manifold. The pressure gauge is marked in both pounds per square inch and gallons or pounds of fuel flow per hour.

### DETONATION

Detonation is the uncontrolled, explosive combustion of fuel. The rate of burning is extremely rapid, producing excessive pressure and temperature within the engine. Detonation can cause the immediate failure of an engine by destroying a piston, valve, or part of the cylinder. Less severe detonation can cause overheating, loss of power, roughness, and reduced engine life.

The causes of detonation can be understood by first examining the normal combustion process, shown in figure 1-26. This figure depicts the inside of a cylinder, as seen through the top of the cylinder head during five phases of compression and combustion.

Normal combustion begins with the spark plugs igniting the fuel-air mixture as it is compressed in the cylinder (item 1). As the piston reaches the end of its compression stroke, two flame fronts are advancing evenly through the unburned fuel-air mixture toward the center of the cylinder (item 2). The fuel is burned in the area immediately behind the advancing flame front, as shown by the heavy lines (item 3). The evenly burning fuel causes a smooth increase in temperature and pressure. This increasing pressure provides the engine with a controlled amount of energy during the piston's power stroke.

*Fig. 1-27. Detonation*

Detonation occurs when the fuel-air mixture is compressed at an abnormally high temperature and/or pressure, as illustrated in figure 1-27. As this mixture is ignited by the spark plugs and the flame front begins to advance across the cylinder, the temperature and pressure within the area of the unburned fuel-air mixture increases still further.

Eventually, the temperature and pressure become great enough to support explosive combustion and the fuel is ignited spontaneously (item 1). The resultant flame fronts advance erratically and rapidly (item 2), creating pressure increases which cause the engine to lose power. The pressure may build to such an extreme that it is in excess of the engine's structural capacity.

The following conditions are common causes of detonation and should be avoided.

1. Takeoff with an overheated engine
2. Operations with an extremely high manifold pressure and extremely low r.p.m.
3. Operations over 75 percent power with an extremely lean mixture

## PREIGNITION

Preignition and detonation are interrelated, since preignition can cause detonation and detonation can cause preignition. Preignition is the premature burning of fuel, caused by a residual hotspot. As shown in figure 1-28, this hotspot can be a glowing piece of carbon deposit on a spark plug (item 1), or a cracked ceramic spark plug insulator.

*Fig. 1-28. Preignition*

The rough edge of a valve, a broken piston ring, cracked piston, or scored cylinder wall may become incandescent and cause preignition (item 2). By the time normal ignition occurs, a large quantity of the fuel-air mixture has already been burned. The premature burning can easily lead to excessive pressures and temperatures. In turn, these factors can result in detonation (item 3).

## EXHAUST GAS TEMPERATURE GAUGE

Some airplanes are equipped with an exhaust gas temperature gauge for each engine to aid in mixture adjustment. The EGT gauge measures the exhaust temperature at a point just outside the combustion chamber. The EGT sensor is a thermocouple-type probe made of dissimilar metals that generate a minute electrical current when heated. This probe is sensitive to temperature changes and provides an accurate means of determining the relative combustion temperatures. Thus, by using the EGT gauge, the mixture control (fuel-air ratio) for each engine can be adjusted with accuracy and efficiency.

After the power is reduced to the cruise power setting, the EGT may be used to lean the mixture. The mixture control is slowly moved toward the lean position while the movement of the EGT needle is noted. As the mixture is leaned, the EGT shows the increase in combustion temperatures. When the peak temperature is reached, the mixture is slowly enriched until a temperature decrease of approximately 50° to 100° Fahrenheit is noted. However, the pilot's operating handbook should be consulted for specific leaning techniques using the EGT gauge.

## ALTERNATE AIR SOURCE

Fuel injection has the added advantage over float carburetion of being less susceptible to induction system icing. The refrigeration process in a carburetor is caused by both the cooling effect of the large pressure reduction in the throttle venturi and the heat loss during the fuel vaporization process. The fuel injection system allows the greatest cooling effect at the cylinder head, where icing is least likely to develop.

The induction air supply in a fuel injection system is filtered prior to entering the induction system air intake. The intake screen at the front of the cowling is a potential source of induction icing. To prevent engine failure due to an iced-over or unusually clogged intake filter, the induction air system of a fuel injected engine must have an alternate air source. The alternate air door may be opened by a manual control located inside the cabin. In addition to the manual control, some engine models have automatic doors which open if the normal air intake becomes obstructed.

# ELECTRICAL SYSTEMS

Electrical power for most light and medium twin-engine airplanes is provided by a 14-volt or a 28-volt, direct current (DC), negative ground system. The generating system incorporates two engine-driven alternators and two voltage regulators. Each alternator circuit has an overvoltage relay which protects the electrical equipment in the event of a voltage regulator malfunction.

Included within the system is the battery, which may be either 12-volt or 24-volt, depending on the requirements of the system. Electrical power from the battery is used primarily for engine starting. However, it is also a source of emergency electrical power in the remote event both alternators should fail.

## SYSTEM COMPONENTS

### ALTERNATORS

The electrical power required by the system is supplied by two engine-driven alternators, one mounted on each engine. The initial electrical power that is produced is alternating current (AC), which is then converted to direct current (DC) for use by the electrical system. If the airplane is equipped with generators, this conversion process is unnecessary because generators initially produce DC electrical power.

Compared to the generator system, the alternator system has an operational advantage, since electrical power is available at lower engine speeds. A generator system requires a minimum engine r.p.m. of approximately 1,000 before the generator provides power to the system. Therefore, during situations when the engine speed is below generator operating speed, all electrical power is supplied by the battery. This condition creates a battery drain, and when the engine speed increases, the battery begins accepting a charge. The numerous cycles of battery charging and discharging over a period of time tend to shorten battery life.

## VOLTAGE REGULATORS

The electrical power supplied by the alternators initially flows through the voltage regulators. A voltage regulator is provided for each alternator and serves two basic functions. First, when both engines are running, both alternators are producing electrical current. The voltage regulators maintain the proper electrical load-sharing between the two alternators. This eliminates one alternator from assuming too great an electrical load while the other has a lesser load. Second, the voltage regulators maintain a constant electrical system voltage. Depending upon the individual airplane and system requirements, the voltage is maintained to either 14.0 or 28.0 volts.

## OVERVOLTAGE RELAYS

After the electrical power passes through the voltage regulator, it is routed to the overvoltage relay. This type of relay is provided within each alternator circuit to protect the electrical system from

overvoltage malfunctions. If a malfunction occurs and the alternator output exceeds the normal 14.0 or 28.0 system voltage, the overvoltage relay trips and the alternator is taken off the line. Most light and medium twin-engine airplanes are equipped with warning lights to indicate that an overvoltage condition has occurred and an alternator is inoperative. If this condition occurs, the pilot's operating handbook should be consulted for the appropriate corrective action.

## BUS BARS AND POWER DISTRIBUTION

Each electrical system incorporates bus bars to distribute the electrical power to each component of the electrical system. Depending upon the airplane's complexity, the number of bars within the electrical system may vary. The following discussion of bus bars and power distribution refers to figure 1-29, which traces electrical power from each alternator to the electrical components of the system.

Electrical power from each alternator passes through the voltage regulators and overvoltage relays enroute to the respective isolation bus bars (item 1). The power is then directed to the left and right electrical power bus bar (item 2). This bus bar divides the electrical power into two different circuits (items 3 and 4). By tracing these two circuits, it is seen that item 3 powers the number 1 bus bar and item 4 powers the number 2 bus bar. Once the electrical power reaches these bars, it is distributed to the individual electrical components on each bus. From the illustration it is seen that the bus bars simply distribute electrical power throughout the system.

In the event one alternator is inoperative, the other alternator will power all the required bus bars, as shown through the circuits of items 3 and 4 in the illustration. The electrical power bus bar in this situation distributes electrical power to both the number 1 and number 2 bus bars and no electrical components

Fig. 1-29. Bus Bars and Power Distribution

are rendered inoperative due to alternator failure. Although not shown in the illustration, the airplane battery may be connected to either or both isolation buses. In the remote event both alternators fail, the battery will power all of the bus bars for a limited period of time.

## CIRCUIT BREAKERS

Circuit breakers are installed to protect each component within the electrical system. In the event a sudden power surge or other malfunction occurs on a circuit, heat is generated and the circuit breaker is tripped automatically. The circuit breaker may be reset after a cooling period by simply pushing it back in place. However, if the breaker trips a second time, it should not be reset or held in place. The corresponding electrical circuit should be considered inoperative and the pilot's operating handbook consulted.

## OPERATION WITH ONE ALTERNATOR INOPERATIVE

In the event one alternator fails or engine-out operations are required, certain considerations must be observed for single alternator operation. During this condition, all unnecessary electrical equipment should be turned off to avoid demanding excess current from the operating alternator. An overloaded alternator may fail and/or trip a circuit breaker.

*Fig. 1-30. Circuit Breakers*

The following method can be used when it is necessary to reduce the electrical load. If the airplane is equipped with 60-ampere alternators, the maximum system load with both alternators operating is 120 amperes. With one alternator inoperative, the maximum system load is 60 amperes. To determine the amperage of each circuit, the pilot can refer to the numbers on circuit breakers as shown in figure 1-30. He should operate only the required equipment that does not have a total of more than 60 amperes. This

procedure precludes the possibility of demanding more amperage than the alternator is capable of producing.

# LANDING GEAR SYSTEMS

The two types of landing gear systems commonly installed on multi-engine airplanes are hydraulic and electric. The difference between the two systems is simply that one uses hydraulic pressure and the other utilizes mechanical linkages from an electric motor to retract or extend the landing gear. Both types of systems incorporate safety features which include an emergency extension provision and a warning horn and lights to alert the pilot of unsafe conditions. Safety switches to prevent inadvertent gear retraction on the ground also are provided on most recently manufactured models.

## HYDRAULIC GEAR SYSTEMS

Hydraulic landing gear systems incorporate either an electrically powered reversible pump or an engine-driven hydraulic pump. Each system uses a hydraulic reservoir and a series of pressure switches to regulate the pressure within the system. When the landing gear selector switch is placed in either the UP or DOWN position, the electrically powered or engine-driven hydraulic pump is put into operation. As shown by the example in figure 1-31, the pump directs hydraulic pressure to each actuating cylinder. As fluid pressure is exerted on one side of the cylinder, fluid on the other side is directed back to the hydraulic pump.

### REGULATION OF SYSTEM PRESSURE

The hydraulic pump, whether it is engine-driven or electrically powered, is designed to operate within a specified pressure range. When excessive pressure is sensed, a relief valve incorporated within the pump opens and hydraulic fluid is routed back to the reservoir.

A second type of relief valve is installed to prevent excessive pressures due to

*Fig. 1-31. Landing Gear Hydraulic System*

thermal expansion. The location of this valve within the system varies between each make and model of airplane.

The hydraulic pressure is also regulated by the limit switches on each of the three landing gear. Each gear has one switch for extension and one switch for retraction. The purpose of these switches is to deenergize the hydraulic pump after the landing gear is either fully extended or retracted. In the event any of the limit switches should fail, a backup valve is installed to relieve excess pressure within the system.

## ELECTRICAL GEAR SYSTEMS

Landing gear systems which are operated electrically utilize a reversible electric motor attached directly to a single gearbox. Each landing gear is connected mechanically to the gearbox through a series of linkages, as shown in figure 1-32. The electric motor is energized when the landing gear selector switch is placed in either the UP or DOWN posi-

tion and the landing gear is driven towards the selected position. The electric motor will continue to operate until the UP or DOWN limit switch on the gearbox disconnects the electrical power. This occurs when the gear is fully retracted or extended.

## LANDING GEAR SAFETY FEATURES

### POSITION LIGHTS

Position lights are common safety features for landing gear systems. The type incorporated in most multi-engine airplanes utilizes four lights—three green and one red. The three green lights indicate that all three landing gear are in the *down and locked* position. The red light illuminates when the gear is in transit or unsafe for landing. Consequently, when the landing gear is cycled up or down, it is normal for the red light to illuminate and then go off when the gear has been fully extended or retracted.

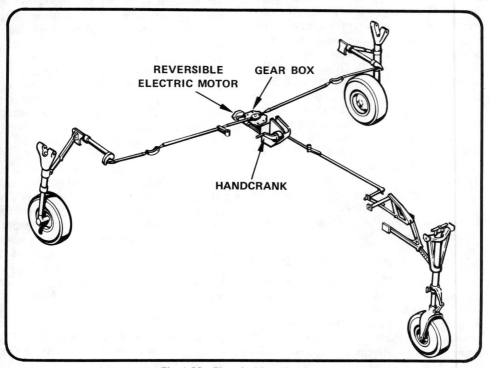

REVERSIBLE ELECTRIC MOTOR  GEAR BOX

HANDCRANK

*Fig. 1-32. Electrical Landing Gear*

### WARNING HORN

A landing gear warning horn is installed to advise the pilot of a potentially hazardous landing gear condition prior to landing. The warning horn also will sound if the landing gear selector switch is in the UP position while the airplane is on the ground. However, the main purpose of the horn is to alert the pilot in the event the gear is retracted or unsafe during the approach to landing.

When power is reduced, a throttle switch located in the power console actuates the warning horn if the landing gear is not down and locked. Generally, this switch is activated at 12 to 14 inches of manifold pressure. The warning horn will continue to operate until the landing gear is down and locked or the power is advanced.

### SAFETY SWITCH

Most currently manufactured multi-engine airplanes are equipped with a landing gear safety switch which prevents the landing gear from retracting while the airplane is on the ground. This switch usually is located on the left main landing gear. A representative type is shown in figure 1-33. In the event the landing gear selector switch is inadvertently placed in the UP position while the airplane is on the ground, the safety switch prevents actuation of the landing gear power source. In this situation, the landing gear will not retract, but the landing gear warning horn will sound, warning the pilot of the improper position of the gear selector switch. Once the selector switch is placed in the proper DOWN position, the warning horn should silence.

### EMERGENCY LANDING GEAR EXTENSION

In the event the power source for landing gear extension fails, an emergency gear *extension* feature is provided for each type of system. The methods of extension include the manual hand pump, $CO_2$ pressure, manual hand crank, or gravity freefall.

*Fig. 1-33. Landing Gear Safety Switch*

Landing gear systems which utilize an engine-driven hydraulic pump to extend the landing gear generally incorporate a manual hand pump. Through use of the hand pump, the pilot can produce system pressure to extend the gear. However, in the event of a leak in the hydraulic system, pressure cannot be maintained with the hand pump. For this reason, an independent $CO_2$ system may be provided on some models as a secondary emergency extension feature. When the system control is pulled, high pressure $CO_2$ flows from a storage cylinder through separate lines to the gear cylinders and forces the landing gear to the extended position. This type of emergency extension should only be used when all other means of lowering the landing gear have failed and when the gear can be left down for landing.

Landing gear systems which normally utilize an electric motor and mechanical linkages to extend the gear incorporate a mechanical hand crank for emergency extension. When extended and engaged for operation, the hand crank is connected to the gearbox and the landing gear may be extended manually by turning the crank. This process normally requires 50 to 55 revolutions of the hand crank.

The last method of emergency extension to be discussed in this section is the gravity freefall system. This type of

Fig. 1-34. Turbocharger System Components

extension system is incorporated in airplanes which utilize hydraulic pressure to hold the landing gear in the retracted position. For this type of gear, the only requirement for extension is to relieve the pressure within the system. An emergency gear extension knob in the cabin controls the freefall valve. The knob can be pulled to release hydraulic pressure so the gear can free fall to the DOWN position. Gravity, in conjunction with aerodynamic loads, extends and locks the gear. The pilot should be aware that if the hydraulic system develops a leak or if hydraulic pressure is relieved for any reason, gravity will cause the landing gear to extend.

# TURBOCHARGING

Control of atmospheric pressure in the induction system goes hand in hand with control of fuel induction and vaporization. Unfortunately, atmospheric pressure varies from location to location and decreases with an increase in altitude. Any decrease in the intake manifold pressure causes a decrease in engine power output. Pressurization of the air in the intake manifold as the airplane climbs to altitude is one solution to this power loss.

## SYSTEM COMPONENTS

The turbocharger consists of two separate components—a compressor and a turbine—connected by a common shaft, as illustrated in figure 1-34. The turbine-driven compressor supplies pressurized air to the engines for high altitude operation. The compressor and its housing are located between the ambient air intake and the induction air manifold. The turbine assembly is part of the exhaust system and utilizes the flow of exhaust gases to drive the compressor.

### WASTEGATE

The automatic wastegate actuator is operated by engine oil pressure and activates a wastegate valve in the exhaust bypass. Oil pressure closes the wastegate and all the exhaust gas is routed into the turbine side of the turbocharger, giving maximum compression to induction air. When the actuator opens the wastegate, a minimum of exhaust gas drives the turbocharger. The balance of the exhaust is dumped overboard. Thus, the wastegate position regulates the compressed air available to the engine.

The following steps illustrate the operation of the system.

1. Induction air is taken in through the air filter and ducted to the compressor.
2. The induction air is then compressed and ducted to the engine.
3. As the wastegate opens, some of the exhaust gases are routed around the turbine, through the exhaust bypass, then overboard.
4. When the wastegate is closed, all of the exhaust gases pass through and drive the turbine, which, in turn, drives the compressor.
5. The exhaust gases are dumped overboard.

### VARIABLE ABSOLUTE PRESSURE CONTROLLER

The control center of the turbocharger system is the variable absolute pressure controller. This device simplifies turbocharging to one control—the throttle. Once the pilot has set the desired manifold pressure, virtually no throttle adjustment is required with changes in altitude. The controller senses manifold pressure requirements for various altitudes and regulates the oil pressure to adjust the wastegate. Thus, the turbocharger maintains only the manifold pressure called for by the throttle setting, except for operation above the critical altitude, where the wastegate reaches the fully closed position. The *critical altitude* is that altitude above which the maximum rated manifold pressure cannot be obtained at full throttle.

## OPERATIONAL CHARACTERISTICS

Aside from the absence of manifold pressure variation with altitude, there is little difference between the turbocharged and the nonturbocharged engine when operated below the critical altitude. Above critical altitude, certain operational characteristics must be understood to fully realize the advantages and capabilities of this turbocharger/ engine combination.

### R.P.M. AND MANIFOLD PRESSURE

Above the critical altitude, any change in r.p.m. results in a change in manifold pressure. When the waste gate is closed, a decrease in r.p.m. normally produces a decrease in manifold pressure. However, with some aircraft, the opposite may be true.

### FUEL FLOW AND MANIFOLD PRESSURE

Above the critical altitude, with r.p.m. and manifold pressure established for cruise, leaning will cause a slight increase in manifold pressure. When the mixture reaches the recommended fuel flow, a slight reduction in manifold pressure may be necessary.

### AIRSPEED AND MANIFOLD PRESSURE

Above the critical altitude, an increase in airspeed will result in a corresponding increase in manifold pressure. This is true because the increase in ram air pressure from an increase in airspeed is magnified by the compressor, resulting in an increase in manifold pressure. The increase in manifold pressure creates a higher airflow through the engine, causing higher turbine speeds and increasing manifold pressure. This characteristic may be used to best advantage by allowing the aircraft to accelerate to cruise speed after leveling off and prior to reducing power.

### ENGINE RESPONSE AT HIGH ALTITUDE

Sudden, large power changes at altitude with rich mixtures can cause loss of engine power. Power changes should be made slowly, with necessary mixture adjustments in a series of two or three steps.

### OVERBOOST CONTROL

The engine incorporates a relief valve in the induction system which is set to relieve any excess manifold pressure that may develop. This valve will open only in the event of a malfunction in the variable absolute pressure control system.

To avoid exceeding normal manifold pressure limits, particularly in cold weather, the last 1-1/2 inches of throttle should be applied slowly while observing manifold pressures. A momentary over-boost to the limit of the relief valve will have no detrimental effect on the engine, but is indicative of a malfunctioning variable absolute pressure controller. If overboost is more than momentary or occurs when engine oil temperature is normal, the controller should be checked at an authorized facility.

# ICE CONTROL EQUIPMENT AND SYSTEMS

The increased need for utilization of aircraft during all weather conditions has led to the development of de-icing and anti-icing equipment. *De-icing* means removal, while *anti-icing* refers to ice prevention. Structural ice control equipment normally is installed to protect the propeller, wing and tail surfaces, windshield, pitot tube, and fuel vents. Some aircraft also make use of shielded antennas to insure adequate reception and transmission, and wing lights to illuminate areas of possible ice accumulation on the wings. The following discussion of ice control equipment, installations, and general operations pertains to systems which are typical of most light and medium twin-engine aircraft used in general aviation.

## ELECTRICAL PROPELLER DE-ICING

The electrical propeller de-icing system employs heating elements to reduce the adhesion between the ice and the propeller. With the system in operation in icing conditions, the heating elements soften the layer of ice adhering to the propeller blades. Centrifugal force and airflow over the propeller cause the ice to be thrown from the blades.

### HEATING ELEMENTS

The heating elements consist of heater wires enclosed in rubber pads. To provide additional strength, the rubber pads

incorporate fabric plies similar to those used in tires. The dull, porous side of the rubber pad is cemented to the leading edge of the propeller blade. The area covered extends from the blade root part way along the leading edge. The outer portion of the heating pad has a very smooth, glossy surface which reduces ice adherence. A propeller with heating pads is shown in figure 1-35.

*Fig. 1-35. Propeller Heat Elements*

The heating pad contains two elements—an inboard heater (near the propeller hub) and an outboard heater. These heating elements are activated individually and cycled on and off periodically by a timer. The cycling process of each heating element allows a slight ice accumulation which normally is removed when the heating cycle is repeated.

### TIMER

In most installations, a timer is used to cycle the electrical current between the right and left propeller heating elements every minute, creating a two-minute cycle. In a given one-minute period, the outboard heaters of the right propeller operate for 30 seconds, followed by a 30-second operation of the inboard heaters. During the next minute, the left propeller heating elements operate in the same manner.

### SLIP RINGS AND BRUSHES

A slip ring and brush assembly is utilized to provide electrical energy to the heat-

*Fig. 1-36. Pneumatic De-Icing System*

ing elements of the rotating propeller. Electricity is transferred by brushes which make contact with the slip ring as the propeller rotates.

### AMMETER

The ammeter in this system provides a means of checking heater operation. In a three-bladed propeller system, the ammeter should indicate approximately 14 to 18 amperes when the system is in use. In addition, the timer cycles every 30 seconds, causing a current fluctuation which is reflected by the ammeter. This fluctuation indicates correct operation.

## WING DE-ICING AND ANTI-ICING EQUIPMENT

Wing de-icing and anti-icing equipment normally falls within two categories— pneumatic boots and heated wings. Pneumatic boots break ice from the wing by expanding and the heated wing pre-

vents ice formation by channeling hot air through the wing's leading edge. The pneumatic system is found primarily on light and medium weight aircraft, while the heated wing system normally is used on jet aircraft.

### PNEUMATIC DE-ICING SYSTEM

A typical pneumatic wing de-icing system is shown in figure 1-36. This system consists of the following components.

1. Inflation boots
2. Timer
3. Pneumatic regulators
4. Engine-driven pressure and vacuum sources

#### Inflation Boots

The inflation boots are fabric-reinforced rubber sheets containing inflation tubes. The boots are cemented to the leading edges of the wings, horizontal stabilizer, and vertical stabilizer. When the de-icing switch is turned on, all of the boots operate simultaneously.

In normal operation, the boots are held in the deflated position by slight vacuum pressure. As the system is energized, approximately 18 p.s.i. of positive pressure is applied to the inflation tubes. This pressure inflates the boots, as shown in figure 1-37, separating the ice from the leading edge. The airflow over the airfoil carries the ice away.

ALL TUBES INFLATED

ALL TUBES DEFLATED

*Fig. 1-37. Pneumatic De-Icing Boots*

The de-icing boots should not be operated until ice has accumulated as specified in the pilot's operating handbook (normally about one-half inch). If the boots are operated with less ice accumulation, they will tend to mold the ice to the new shape, rather than breaking it from the surface. If this occurs, ice will accumulate on the contour formed by the inflated boot, and further operation of the de-icing system will have no effect.

## Timer

When the de-icing switch is activated, the timer energizes the pneumatic pressure control valves for five to eight seconds. During this interval, pressure is applied to the inflation tubes, resulting in expansion of boots. Then, the timer automatically deenergizes the control valves, permitting the pressurized air to be exhausted overboard. The cycle is completed when a vacuum is reapplied to the boots, holding them in the deflated position.

## Pneumatic Regulators

Pneumatic regulators are the heart of the wing de-icing system. Through a network of solenoids and control valves, the regulators govern the pressure and distribution of air in the system. The pneumatic regulators also control the pressure for the airplane instruments and other aircraft equipment.

## Pressure and Vacuum Source

The wing de-icing system utilizes a pneumatic pump located on each engine. In case of a single pump failure, the remaining pump will supply adequate pressure and vacuum to operate the gyro flight instruments and wing de-icing systems.

## HEATED WING ANTI-ICING SYSTEM

The heated wing anti-icing system often is found on turbojet or turboprop aircraft because the jet engine has a ready source of hot air to heat the wing. In this system, hot air is bled from one of the later stages of the compressor section of the engine and channeled to the aircraft wings.

The leading edge is enclosed and becomes a heated chamber. As the hot air from the engines flows through this chamber, it warms the leading edge to a temperature above freezing, preventing ice formation. A typical heated wing is illustrated in figure 1-38.

HOT AIR SOURCES

EXHAUST

HOT AIR DUCT

*Fig. 1-38. Heated Wing Anti-Icing System*

## ELECTRICALLY HEATED WINDSHIELD

Most aircraft are equipped with a defroster consisting of vents which direct hot air across the windshield on the inside of the cabin. Although this system is adequate for some operations, flight in icing conditions may cause ice to adhere to the windshield, severly restricting visibility. The electrically heated windshield has been developed to combat this problem.

In this system, heat wires are embedded either in the windshield or in a piece of transparent material which is bonded to the windshield. In either system, electrical current flowing through the wires heats the windshield and prevents ice formation. To prevent overheating of the windshield, the system should be operated only during flight. If the windshield overheats, it may become "milky" in appearance and greatly reduce visibility.

## OPERATION OF ICE CONTROL EQUIPMENT

Both anti-icing and de-icing equipment should be checked prior to flight whenever icing conditions are anticipated. In addition to ground checks, the pilot should cycle the wing de-icing boots and visually check for correct operation. During this time, the electric propeller de-icer can be turned on and the ammeter observed for proper indications. The prevention (anti-icing) equipment should be turned on prior to entering icing conditions or at the first indication of icing. This is necessary because most anti-icing equipment must "heat up" to normal operating temperatures before it is effective.

# CABIN HEATING SYSTEMS

Although the components of each heating, ventilating, and defrosting system are basically identical, differences are found in the two methods of heat origination and regulation. The first type of system incorporates a gasoline combustion type heater and the second uses a simple heat exchanger mounted on each engine exhaust manifold.

## GASOLINE COMBUSTION HEATER

The gasoline combustion heater is used on some makes and models of twin-engine airplanes as the source of cabin heat. The heater is usually located in the nose of the airplane and receives its fuel supply from the airplane fuel system.

Fresh air enters through the nose of the airplane and is routed through the heater. When the airplane is on the ground, a fan forces the heated air to the heat outlets or the defroster ducts in the cabin. After takeoff, the fan is deactivated automatically when the landing gear is retracted, and ram air provides heat circulation.

A thermostat usually is located in the duct just aft of the heater. When the temperature of the heated air exceeds the setting of the thermostat, it opens automatically and shuts off the heater. When the heated air cools to the thermostat setting, the heater starts again. Thus, the heater cycles on and off to maintain an even air temperature.

## MANIFOLD HEAT EXCHANGER

In other models, cabin and defrost heat is provided by a heat exchanger mounted on the exhaust manifold of each engine. Outside air enters the system through a scoop on the engine cowling, passes through the heat exchanger, and is heated by the exhaust manifold. A combination heater and defroster valve, located in the forward side of the firewall, directs heated air for the cabin interior through a fresh air and temperature control valve assembly. At this point in the system, the temperature is regulated before the heat enters the cabin interior. This regulation is not accomplished by an automatic thermostat, but rather, by adding cool, outside air to the heated air.

A manual control inside the airplane regulates the amount of outside air mixed with the heated air. The heated air that is routed through the heat and defroster valve for defrosting purposes does not go through the temperature control valve assembly. It is passed directly from the heat and defroster valve to the defroster outlet located at the base of the windshield. The defroster has a separate control lever that can be turned off when its operation is not required. When both the cabin heat and the defroster controls are off, heated air from the heat exchanger is dumped overboard.

## SUPPLEMENTAL OXYGEN

There are three basic types of oxygen equipment, a *continuous-flow* system, a *diluter demand* system, and a *pressure-demand* system. For the most part, these systems have a similar design. The most common oxygen system used in general aviation aircraft is the *continuous-flow* system and can provide adequate oxygen up to an altitude of 25,000 feet. Above 17,000 feet, a tight mask seal must be maintained.

The second type is the *diluter-demand* system, which increases the utility of the basic continuous-flow equipment by conserving oxygen at lower altitudes and increasing the oxygen flow at higher altitudes. This type of system is required above 25,000 feet and incorporates a second regulator in the mask or hose assembly. Most of these systems automatically furnish more oxygen as altitude increases. The regulators normally provide 100% oxygen by approximately 30,000 feet. However, 100% oxygen can be set at any time. The mask must have an airtight seal and can be used safely up to 35,000 feet.

The third type is the *pressure-demand* oxygen system and is used for flights above 35,000 feet. This system delivers pressurized oxygen to the lungs. Because oxygen is supplied under positive pressure, breathing is relaxed during the inhale while positive pressure from the oxygen system fills the lungs. To exhale, effort must be exerted against the positive pressure.

All aircraft oxygen systems must use *aviator's breathing oxygen.* Specifications for this type of oxygen are 99.5% pure oxygen and not more than .005 milligrams of water per liter. Medical oxygen contains too much moisture, which can collect in the valves and lines of the system and freeze.

## CABIN PRESSURIZATION

The pressurization system on most turbocharged aircraft uses compressed air from the compressor side of the turbocharger. Since the compression of air in the turbocharger generates considerable heat, a heat exchanger cools the air to the desired temperature before it actually enters the cabin. The heat exchanger is exposed to the outside air by an airscoop or inlet. After the hot, compressed air is cooled in the heat exchanger, system components route it to the cabin. During cold weather operations, a mixer valve routes hot, compressed air directly from the turbocharger to the blower of the ventilation system rather than the heat exchanger. From the ventilation blower, air is routed through the cabin heat and defroster outlets.

There are two types of pressurization systems used in general aviation, they are a *basic system* and a *controllable system*. A *basic system* automatically begins pressurizing the cabin as the aircraft climbs through a preset altitude. Although this altitude may vary with different manufacturers, 8,000 feet is commonly used. As the aircraft continues to climb, the cabin pressure altitude remains at 8,000 feet until reaching approximately 20,000 feet. Above this altitude, the maximum differential pressure is achieved and the cabin pressure slowly decreases. The maximum differential pressure is normally in the range of 3.35 to 4.5 p.s.i. The basic system is easy to operate. The system is simply activated before the flight.

A *controllable system*, as shown in figure 1-39, is quite different from a basic system because the altitude at which pressurization begins can be set. The outer scale on the cabin altitude and differential pressure indicator (item 1) shows the pressure altitude in the cabin. The inner scale indicates the pressure differential between the cabin and the atmosphere. The cabin rate-of-climb indicator (item 2) shows a climb or descent when below the selected altitude or above the maximum differential pressure altitude. At the current setting, the airplane can maintain a cabin pressure of about 6,300 feet while it is at or below 14,500 feet. The cabin altitude selector (item 3) sets the altitude at which pressurization begins. Normally the cabin altitude selector is set 1,000 feet above the field elevation of the departure or destination airport, whichever is highest. An electrical switch (item 4) controls the safety dump valve. When it is in the ON position, it closes the valve and pressurizes the cabin. When the pressure dump valve (item 5) is pulled, it opens and allows pressurization air to flow overboard.

Additional safety features normally include an outflow valve and a safety valve. The outflow valve functions automatically and exhausts used cabin air at a controlled rate to maintain the desired cabin altitude. The safety valve is controlled from the instrument panel and is used for normal decompression. It also prevents the cabin altitude from exceeding the preset differential between the cabin air and outside air in the event the outflow valve fails in the closed position. Refer to the pilot's operating handbook for specific system operating procedures.

With all of the safety devices on pressurization systems, rapid decompression, or even a gradual loss of cabin pressure, seldom occurs. In spite of this, the con-

*Fig 1-39. Controllable Pressurization System*

sequences of a rapid decompression at high altitudes must be considered. *Time of useful consciousness* is the term used to describe the maximum time a person has to make a rational, lifesaving decision and carry it out after a loss of oxygen. Figure 1-40 illustrates how the time of useful consciousness varies with altitude and the level of activity. For example, with moderate activity at a cabin pressure altitude of 20,000 feet, a person without supplemental oxygen has 5 minutes to carry out a saving decision. Above 30,000 feet, the time of useful consciousness during moderate activity decreases to 45 seconds. If a rapid decompression occurs at a high altitude, the pilot must immediately don the oxygen mask, select 100% oxygen, and make a rapid descent to an appropriate lower altitude.

| TIME OF USEFUL CONSCIOUSNESS | | |
|---|---|---|
| Altitude | Sitting Quietly | Moderate Activity |
| 40,000 Ft. | 30 Sec. | 18 Sec. |
| 35,000 Ft. | 45 Sec. | 30 Sec. |
| 30,000 Ft. | 1 Min. and 15 Sec. | 45 Sec. |
| 25,000 Ft. | 3 Min. | 2 Min. |
| 22,000 Ft. | 10 Min. | 5 Min. |
| 20,000 Ft. | 12 Min. | 5 Min. |

*Fig 1-40. Time of Useful Consciousness*

# chapter 2

# PERFORMANCE CONSIDERATIONS

## INTRODUCTION

Weight, balance, and performance information for multi-engine airplanes is more extensive and generally more complex than for single-engine airplanes. For this reason, it is essential that applicants for the multi-engine rating be thoroughly familiar with performance considerations. This chapter points out the distinctive aspects of multi-engine weight and balance control and illustrates the charts and tables which are necessary for determining various performance values.

---

NOTE:
*This chapter contains a cross section of multi-engine charts and tables. They include some charts with temperatures in degrees Fahrenheit and speed in miles per hour, as well as newer formats which use degrees Celsius and knots. These examples are for instructional purposes only and should not be used for flight planning. The appropriate pilot's operating handbook should be consulted for specific weight and balance computations and performance data.*

---

## SECTION A—WEIGHT AND BALANCE

Flight operations must be conducted within the weight and balance limitations imposed by the manufacturer. When either weight or balance exceed limits, performance cannot be accurately predicted. Since neither the manufacturer nor the FAA can provide reliable performance data when certification limits are exceeded, the weight and balance condition of an airplane should be checked carefully prior to departure.

### WEIGHT

There are several *standard aircraft weights* designated for weight and balance computations. However, there is some diversity in terminology based on the various manufacturers' preferences or the particular period of manufacture. For the purposes of this discussion, the following aircraft weights are considered.

1. Maximum ramp weight
2. Maximum takeoff weight
3. Maximum landing weight
4. Maximum zero fuel weight
5. Basic empty weight

*Maximum ramp weight*, when applicable, is the approved weight that assures ground maneuverability. It includes the fuel weight required for engine start, taxi, and warm-up. The *maximum takeoff weight* is the highest weight approved for the start of the takeoff run. The *maximum landing weight* is the highest weight approved for landing touchdown and is generally based on the strength of the landing gear or related structural components.

A *maximum zero fuel weight* is applicable on some airplanes to limit the ratio of loads between the fuselage and wings. The maximum load that an airplane can carry also depends on the way the load is distributed. The weight of an airplane in flight is supported largely by the wings; therefore, as the load carried in the fuselage is increased, the bending moment on the wings is increased. An airplane might safely carry 2,000 pounds if 1,400 pounds were carried in the fuselage and 600 pounds of fuel were in the wings. However, 2,000 pounds might be an unsafe load if the weight distribution were 1,600 pounds in the fuselage and 400 pounds in the wings. The excessive bending moment imposed on the wings by the 1,600 pounds in the fuselage might exceed the strength of related structural components. During preflight planning, particularly for larger multi-engine aircraft, the expected fuel burnoff should be calculated to ensure that the airplane's weight distribution remains within limits throughout the flight. By observing the maximum zero fuel weight, a safe

ratio of loads between the fuselage and wings can be maintained.

The *basic empty weight* includes the weight of a standard airplane, all optional equipment, unusable fuel, and full operating fluids, including full oil. This is the most convenient weight for beginning weight and balance computations.

NOTE:
*Airplanes manufactured in past years may specify a licensed empty weight rather than a basic empty weight. Licensed empty weight does not include full oil. When operating such an airplane, the oil weight must be added to the licensed empty weight to determine the basic empty weight. Many aviation publications also use the general term, gross weight, to describe the total aircraft weight at a given time.*

## WEIGHT COMPUTATIONS

The following items are typically used to compute weight.

1. Basic empty weight
2. Payload
   a. Occupants (crew and passengers)
   b. Baggage/cargo
3. Usable fuel

The basic empty weight is found in the weight and balance records. The sample record in figure 2-1 reflects the continuous history of changes in airplane structure and/or equipment that affect the weight and balance of the airplane. The latest entry for basic empty weight should be used. After this weight is located, it is entered in reference 1 of the weight and balance form, as shown in figure 2-2.

The *payload* normally consists of the occupants/cargo and baggage. It is always best to use the actual weight of the pilot and passengers for a flight, especially when close to the weight and balance limits. However, in the absence of actual weights, the following guidelines may be used: 170 pounds for an

## WEIGHT AND BALANCE RECORD

(CONTINUOUS HISTORY OF CHANGES IN STRUCTURE OR EQUIPMENT
AFFECTING WEIGHT AND BALANCE)

| DATE | ITEM | | DESCRIPTION OF ARTICLE OR MODIFICATION | WEIGHT CHANGE | | | | | | BASIC EMPTY WEIGHT | |
| | IN | OUT | | ADDED (+) | | | REMOVED (−) | | | | |
| | | | | WT. (LB) | ARM (IN) | MOMENT /100 | WT. (LB) | ARM (IN) | MOMENT /100 | WT (LB) | MOMENT /100 |
|---|---|---|---|---|---|---|---|---|---|---|---|
| 5/27 | | | BASIC EMPTY WT | | | | | | | 3464.2 | 1223.3 |
| 8/3 | | X | ALTIMETER, FT & MILLIBARS LH | | | | 1.1 | 13.5 | .15 | 3463.1 | 1223.2 |
| 8/3 | X | | 400 ENCODING ALTIMETER − IN | 2.6 | 13.0 | .34 | | | | 3465.7 | 1223.5 |
| 8/3 | X | | 400 GLIDE SLOPE INSL | 2.9 | -50.0 | -1.45 | | | | 3468.6 | 1222.1 |
| 8/3 | X | | RECEIVER R-443B | 2.4 | -63.0 | -1.51 | | | | 3471.0 | 1220.6 |
| 8/3 | X | | MOUNT 36450 | 0.9 | -63.0 | -.57 | | | | 3471.9 | 1220.0 |
| 8/3 | X | | ANTENNA RGS-10-48 | 0.1 | -92.0 | -.09 | | | | 3472.0 | 1220.1 |

OLD BASIC EMPTY WEIGHT 3,464.2 — OLD TOTAL MOMENT 122,330 — OLD CG 35.31 IN.
NEW BASIC EMPTY WEIGHT 3,472.0 — NEW TOTAL MOMENT 122,010 — NEW CG 35.14 IN.

*Fig. 2-1. Weight and Balance Record*

adult with an average physical stature and 80 pounds for children between the ages of 2 and 12. The actual weights for baggage and cargo must be used, since it is impossible to formulate a standard weight. These computations are made on the left side of the weight and balance form, as illustrated in figure 2-2. After the payload is totaled, it is transferred to reference 2 and added to the basic empty weight. This provides the zero fuel weight, or total weight before fuel

## SAMPLE WEIGHT AND BALANCE FORM

| PAYLOAD COMPUTATIONS | | | | REF | ITEM | | WEIGHT | MOMENT/100 |
|---|---|---|---|---|---|---|---|---|
| ITEM OCCUPANTS OR CARGO | ARM | WEIGHT | MOMENT/100 | 1. | BASIC EMPTY WEIGHT | | 3,472 | |
| | | | | 2. | PAYLOAD | | 800 | |
| Seat 1 | | 190 | | 3. * | ZERO FUEL WEIGHT (sub-total) (Do not exceed maximum zero fuel weight) | | 4,272 | |
| Seat 2 | | 150 | | | | | | |
| Seat 3 | | 170 | | | | | | |
| Seat 4 | | 150 | | 4. | FUEL LOADING | (main) | 600 | |
| Seat 5 | | — | | | | (auxiliary) | 378 | |
| Seat 6 | | — | | | | (wing lockers) | - - - | |
| BAGGAGE | | 140 | | 5. * | TAKEOFF WEIGHT | | 5,250 | |
| PAYLOAD | | 800 | | | | | | |
| | | | | 6. | LESS FUEL TO DESTINATION | (main) | 155 | |
| | | | | | | (auxiliary) | 378 | |
| | | | | | | (wing lockers) | - - - | |
| | | | | 7. * | LANDING WEIGHT | | 4,717 | |

*Fig. 2-2. Weight and Balance Form*

loading, as depicted in reference 3. This value should not exceed the maximum zero fuel weight specified in the pilot's operating handbook. Any weight in excess of this amount must be comprised of fuel.

The total weight of the usable fuel is determined by multiplying the number of gallons by six pounds. Once computed, the fuel weight is entered in reference 4. The final figure for takeoff weight is found by totaling the zero fuel weight and fuel loading items, as determined in reference 5. The landing weight is determined by subtracting the fuel required to fly to the destination. Once the weight and balance form is complete, the takeoff weight is checked against the maximum takeoff weight in the limitations section of the pilot's operating handbook to insure the airplane is loaded within limits.

### ADJUSTING WEIGHT

If the maximum allowable weight limit is exceeded, it must be reduced prior to flight and before a check can be made of the center of gravity. There are three items of the useful load which can be varied to reduce weight—fuel, passengers, and baggage/cargo.

The selection of one or more of these possibilities depends on the flight requirements. If conditions are such that all passengers and their baggage need to go on the flight, the fuel requirements must be calculated carefully and reduced to the minimum required for safe operation.

It is important to realize that in addition to being a legal limit, a specified maximum weight is also a limit on airplane capability. Attempting flight with the airplane loaded above this limit not only violates Federal Aviation Regulations, but it reduces or eliminates built-in safety margins.

Loading an airplane above the maximum weight adversely affects performance. Takeoff roll is longer and climb performance is severely reduced; in fact, the airplane may not be able to climb out of ground effect. Cruise requires a higher angle of attack, stall speed is higher, approach speed must be greater, and landing roll is longer. In addition, the engines must operate continuously at higher power settings, increasing the possibility of overheating or a component failure.

All of these factors clearly indicate that flight should not be attempted when an airplane is loaded above its maximum weight. At best, the airplane is being flown under conditions for which no performance data are available. In this situation, structural damage may occur even during normal maneuvers. Also, a malfunction, such as loss of power, could easily result in a situation from which a safe recovery is doubtful.

## BALANCE

There are several terms which are used when making balance computations. They are included in the following list.

1. Center of gravity
2. Reference datum
3. Arm
4. Moment

The *center of gravity* (CG) is the point at which an airplane would balance if suspended. Its distance from the reference datum is found by dividing the total moment, explained below, by the total weight of the airplane.

The *reference datum* is an imaginary vertical plane from which all horizontal distances are measured for balance purposes. The datum location is arbitrarily specified by the manufacturer. It may be at the firewall, the nose, or a point in space in front of the aircraft. In any case, it lies along the longitudinal axis. Regardless of the placement, all moments aft of the datum have positive values, while all moments forward of this reference have negative values.

*Fig. 2-3. Arm*

An *arm* is the horizontal distance from the reference datum to the center of gravity of an item, as illustrated in figure 2-3. For example, if a suitcase were placed in the baggage compartment 126 inches aft of the datum, it would have an arm of 126.

The *moment* is the product of the weight of an item multiplied by its arm. If the suitcase in the previous example weighed 25 pounds, it would have a moment of 3,150 pound-inches.

As long as these factors are used to insure the airplane is loaded within the CG limits designated by the manufacturer, all performance and flight characteristics will be normal. The airplane will be stable in flight and responsive to the controls. However, improper loading can cause detrimental flight effects.

## FORWARD CG EFFECTS

An airplane that is loaded with the CG forward of limits requires a greater amount of elevator or stabilator pressure to break ground on takeoff. During climb and cruise flight, the additional back pressure required will decrease the cruise speed and climb capabilities. On a landing approach, an airplane loaded forward of limits may contact the ground with the nosewheel before the main gear, even though full aft elevator or stabilator control is used.

## AFT CG EFFECTS

A CG located aft of the approved CG range is the most hazardous condition. The airplane becomes tail heavy and very unstable in pitch, regardless of its airspeed. If the CG is too far aft, it may not be possible to raise the tail and lower the nose because of reduced control effectiveness. This condition may result in a pitch up and stall, especially during slow speed operations such as takeoff or landing.

## CENTER OF GRAVITY COMPUTATIONS

There are several methods in common use for determining an airplane's center of gravity. Since the basic computation method generally is considered too cumbersome for multi-engine airplanes, this discussion will be limited to the following list.

1. Tabular method
2. Graph method
3. Computer/plotter method

### TABULAR METHOD

The *tabular method* utilizes weight and moment tables like those shown in figure 2-4. These tables are found in the pilot's operating handbook or the weight and balance papers. Once the information is

Fig. 2-4. Weight and Moment Tables

obtained from the table, it is transferred to a weight and balance form similar to the one depicted in figure 2-5.

First, the weight of each item is entered and the arms are determined from the passenger seat and baggage diagram. Next, the weight and moment tables are used to determine the total moment. On these tables, the moment values are divided by 100 to reduce the size of the numbers. Finally, the total moment is divided by the total weight to determined the CG location (212,800 lb.-in. ÷ 5,250 lbs. = 40.5 in.)

Now that the CG has been computed, it is necessary to determine if it is within prescribed limits, as indicated by the shaded area of figure 2-6. Since the CG computed was 40.5 inches at a gross weight of 5,250 pounds, it is within limits.

### GRAPH METHOD

Another approach to computing the center of gravity is the *graph method*. The moments on the loading graph shown in figure 2-7 are divided by 1,000, making the information easy to read and use. The loading graph is an alternative

## SAMPLE WEIGHT AND BALANCE FORM

| PAYLOAD COMPUTATIONS | | | | R E F | ITEM | | WEIGHT | MOMENT/ 100 |
|---|---|---|---|---|---|---|---|---|
| ITEM OCCUPANTS OR CARGO | ARM | WEIGHT | MOMENT/ 100 | 1. | BASIC EMPTY WEIGHT | | 3472 | 1220 |
| | | | | 2. | PAYLOAD | | 800 | 520 |
| Seat 1 | 37 | 190 | 70 | 3. | * ZERO FUEL WEIGHT (sub-total) (Do not exceed maximum zero fuel weight) | | 4272 | 1740 |
| Seat 2 | 37 | 150 | 56 | | | | | |
| Seat 3 | 68 | 170 | 116 | | | | | |
| Seat 4 | 68 | 150 | 102 | 4. | FUEL LOADING | (main) | 600 | 210 |
| Seat 5 | | | | | | (auxiliary) | 378 | 178 |
| Seat 6 | | | | | | (wing lockers) | --- | --- |
| BAGGAGE | 126 | 140 | 176 | 5. | * TAKEOFF WEIGHT | | 5250 | 2128 |
| PAYLOAD | --- | 800 | 520 | 6. | LESS FUEL TO DESTINATION | (main) | 155 | 54 |
| | | | | | | (auxiliary) | 378 | 178 |
| | | | | | | (wing lockers) | --- | --- |
| | | | | 7. | * LANDING WEIGHT | | 4717 | 1896 |

*Fig. 2-5. Weight and Balance Form*

to the tabular method for determining moments.

The graph is used by entering it at the appropriate weight on the left, proceeding horizontally to the appropriate reference line, and then vertically down to read the moment/1,000 pound-inches. In figure 2-7, for example, the graph is entered at 340 pounds (item 1), the weight of the pilot and front seat passenger. This point is extended horizontally until it intersects the pilot and front passenger line (item 2). The moment of

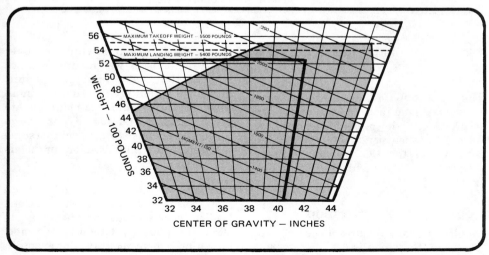

*Fig. 2-6. Center of Gravity Graph*

LOADING GRAPH

*Fig. 2-7. Loading Graph*

29.1 is read directly below this point (item 3).

This procedure is repeated for each individual item and the moments are recorded on the weight and balance form. The weights and moments then are totaled and the CG is determined by dividing the total moment by the total weight.

### COMPUTER/PLOTTER METHOD

Another method requires a special computer/plotter which is designed for use with a specific type of airplane. This device has several advantages over other methods of weight and balance computations. For example, weight and CG location are determined simultaneously. In addition, calculations are much quicker and usually are more accurate because long, cumbersome multiplication and division problems are eliminated.

One side of the weight and balance plotter usually provides a list of general loading recommendations which initially allow the pilot to determine the most logical placement of loads. For example, when four people occupy the airplane,

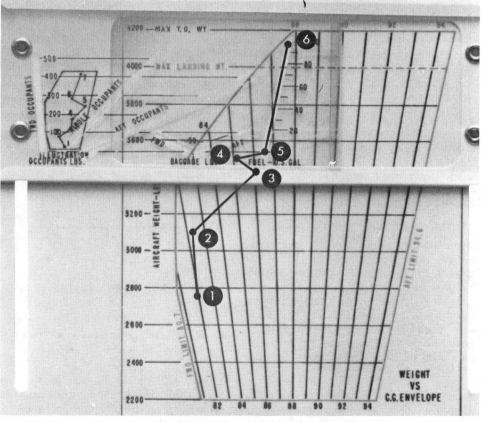

Fig. 2-8. Weight and Balance Plotter

the recommended loading may place two in the front seats and two in the middle seats. Similar recommendations for baggage and fuel loads also are specified.

The computation side of the weight and balance plotter is depicted in figure 2-8. This slide is precut with slots representing the total weight of the forward, middle, and aft occupants; the baggage in the forward and aft compartments; and the fuel in U.S. gallons. By marking through the slots onto the envelope, the effect on CG location for each compartment can be determined progressively.

Figure 2-8 also illustrates the solution to a typical problem under the following conditions.

Basic empty weight  . . . . . 2,745 lbs.
Empty weight CG  . . . . . . . 82.0 in.

Pilot and front passenger  . . 340 lbs.
Center seat passengers  . . . . 340 lbs.
Forward baggage . . . . . . . . 50 lbs.
Aft baggage  . . . . . . . . . . 50 lbs.
Fuel (95-gal. maximum)  . . . 570 lbs.

The steps for solving this problem include the following items which correspond to the callouts in figure 2-8.

1.  Locate the basic empty weight and
    center of gravity
2.  Plot pilot and front passenger
3.  Plot center seat passengers
4.  Plot forward baggage
5.  Plot aft baggage
6.  Plot fuel

The weight and CG location fall within the envelope; therefore, the airplane
meets weight and balance requirements. Additionally, as the fuel is
used, the weight and CG will follow
down the fuel line and stay within the
envelope for landing.

### CENTER OF GRAVITY SHIFT

After making weight and balance computations, the pilot may find that, although the airplane is within specified
weight limits, the CG range has been
exceeded. In this case, the load must
be shifted to return the airplane to a
safe flight condition. This is usually
accomplished by shifting the passengers and/or baggage to more favorable locations.

A typical example might involve an
airplane loaded to 4,000 pounds with a
computed CG of 96.1 inches. If the aft
CG limit is 94.6 inches, the CG is 1.5
inches aft of the limit. Since the aft
CG limit is exceeded, the *total aircraft
moment must be reduced*. If the forward CG limit had been exceeded, it
would have been necessary to *increase
total aircraft moment*.

Total aircraft moment may be reduced
by moving weight forward. Assuming
the airplane in this example has both
a forward and aft baggage compartment, some of the baggage in the aft
compartment could be moved to the
forward compartment. As an example,
if the distance between the two compartments is 156 inches, the amount
of weight to be moved is calculated
with the following weight formula:

$$\frac{\text{Weight of Cargo Moved}}{\text{Weight of Airplane}} = \frac{\text{Distance CG Moves}}{\text{Distance Between Arm Locations}}$$

Substituting the known values in the
equation results in the following calculations:

1)  $\dfrac{\text{Weight of Cargo Moved}}{4{,}000} = \dfrac{1.5}{156}$

2)  $156 \times \text{Weight of Cargo Moved} = 6{,}000$

3)  Weight of Cargo Moved = 6,000 ÷
    156, or 38.5 lbs.

Therefore, to load the airplane within
acceptable limits, 38.5 pounds must be
moved from the aft compartment to
the forward compartment. This is a
*minimum* value that will result in the
airplane being loaded at the aft CG
limit. For better overall aircraft control during flight, the pilot should consider moving additional weight in order to move the CG to a more favorable position.

# SECTION B—PERFORMANCE CHARTS

Through an approved pilot's operating handbook, manufacturers provide all of the performance information necessary to insure safe operation of an airplane. It is important for the prospective multi-engine pilot to become thoroughly familiar with the data this handbook contains. Concepts such as the accelerate-stop distance and single-engine climb performance are unique to multi-engine operations, and accurate computations of these and other values are important to safe operation.

## PERFORMANCE FACTORS

There are several factors which affect aircraft performance, including density altitude, surface wind, runway condition, and gross weight. Normally, density altitude is the most significant factor because of its effect on engine performance, propeller efficiency, and lift generated by the wings.

### DENSITY ALTITUDE

Density altitude is pressure altitude corrected for temperature deviations from the standard atmosphere. A pressure altitude of 29.92 inches of mercury at sea level and a temperature of 15° Celsius (59° Fahrenheit) are used to represent the standard atmosphere. These values are used by some manufacturers as a basis for plotting performance data. Under the newer performance chart formats, density altitude may not be used, since tables or graphs can be presented with pressure altitude and temperature in degrees Celsius. Essentially, these charts combine the density altitude problem with the performance problem.

### DENSITY ALTITUDE DETERMINATION

When necessary, density altitude may be determined by using either a chart presentation or a computer. For example, when using a chart like the one shown in

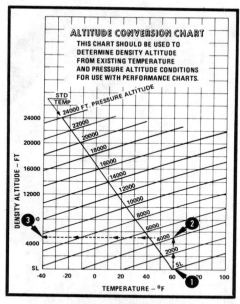

*Fig. 2-9. Density Altitude Chart*

figure 2-9, the first step is to enter the chart at the appropriate temperature. A temperature of 60° Fahrenheit and a pressure altitude of 4,000 feet are used for this example. The 60° Fahrenheit line (item 1) is followed upward to the diagonal line representing a 4,000-foot pressure altitude (item 2). The density altitude is then determined by moving to the left margin of the chart and reading 5,000 feet (item 3).

Another way to determine the density altitude is by using a computer. Referring to figure 2-10, the 60° Fahrenheit temperature is converted to 16° Celsius (item 1), since the computer requires use of degrees Celsius for density altitude computations. This temperature is placed opposite the pressure altitude of 4,000 feet (item 2). The resulting density altitude of 5,000 feet appears in the density altitude window (item 3).

### HUMIDITY

Although humidity normally is not included in density altitude computations,

Fig. 2-10. Computer Solution

Since the wind seldom blows precisely down the runway, it often is necessary to determine the actual headwind component. This can be accomplished using a wind component chart.

## RUNWAY CONDITIONS

Runway conditions are also a factor in takeoff performance, since most takeoff values are based on using a fully loaded airplane on a hard-surfaced, dry, level runway. Uphill gradients and soft or wet surfaces decrease takeoff performance. On the other hand, downhill gradients and hard or dry surfaces improve takeoff performance.

## WEIGHT

Weight is another significant factor that affects takeoff and climb performance. The takeoff performance information found on most light, single-engine airplane charts is based on maximum weight, since all conditions at a lesser weight will improve airplane performance. However, multi-engine performance information normally specifies additional weights which are less than the maximum weight to more accurately determine performance values when the airplane is operated at lighter weights.

# PERFORMANCE CHARTS

Performance charts in the pilot's operating handbook provide a method of determining airplane performance for a given set of conditions. Although these charts vary in design between manufacturers, they generally are presented in either tabular or graphic displays. They also are presented to correspond to the normal chronological sequence of flight events.

## TAKEOFF CHARTS

Takeoff charts follow the general information in the pilot's operating handbook and normally are quite detailed. A typical multi-engine takeoff chart is shown

it should be noted that water vapor will increase takeoff distance and decrease climb performance. The rated horsepower of an engine is determined in dry air and standard atmospheric conditions. For this reason, as water vapor increases, air density decreases and the engine's power output decreases. This power loss can be as high as seven percent when the relative humidity is 100 percent.

## SURFACE WIND

The surface wind direction and velocity also have a direct bearing on takeoff performance. Substantial headwinds shorten the takeoff run and compensate for some of the adverse effects of high density altitude. Conversely, a tailwind increases the takeoff run because a higher groundspeed is required for takeoff.

Fig. 2-11. 0° Flap Takeoff Ground Roll

in figure 2-11. From this chart, the pilot can determine the ground run required for a normal takeoff. A sample problem is based on the following conditions.

Flap configuration ................. 0°
Temperature ...................... 8°C
Pressure altitude ............... 680 ft.
Takeoff weight .............. 3,430 lbs.
Headwind component ........... 6 kts.
Liftoff speed.................. 71 KIAS

The following procedure should be used to determine the ground run required for takeoff. The steps correspond to the numbered callouts on the chart.

❶ Enter the chart at the outside air temperature line.

❷ Move vertically to the appropriate pressure altitude line.

❸ Move horizontally to the 3,800-pound maximum weight line.

❹ Move diagonally to the actual airplane weight line of 3,430 pounds.

❺ Move horizontally to the 0-knot line.

❻ Move diagonally to the actual headwind component line of 6 knots.

❼ Move horizontally to the ground roll distance of 820 feet.

## ACCELERATE-STOP DISTANCE

Another important consideration when computing takeoff data is the accelerate-stop distance. This distance is the amount of runway required under existing conditions to accelerate to liftoff speed, experience an engine failure at that point, immediately discontinue the takeoff, and bring the airplane to a full stop. A typical accelerate-stop distance chart is depicted in figure 2-12. The dashed line indicates the solution to a sample problem, based on the information at the top of the chart and on the following conditions.

Weight.................4,300 lbs.
Engine failure speed ...... 81 KIAS
Pressure altitude .......... 2,000 ft.
Temperature ................. 20°C

## ACCELERATE STOP DISTANCE

CONDITIONS:
1. Power - FULL THROTTLE and 2700 RPM Before Brake Release.
2. Mixtures - LEAN for field elevation.
3. Wing Flaps - UP.
4. Cowl Flaps - OPEN.
5. Level, Hard Surface, Dry Runway.
6. Engine Failure at Engine Failure Speed.
7. Idle Power and Heavy Braking After Engine Failure.
NOTE:
1. If full power is applied without brakes set, distances apply from point where full power is applied.
2. Decrease distance 3% for each 4 knots headwind.
3. Increase distance 5% for each 2 knots tailwind.

| WEIGHT · POUNDS | ENGINE FAILURE SPEED · KIAS | PRESSURE ALTITUDE · FEET | TOTAL DISTANCE - FEET | | | | |
|---|---|---|---|---|---|---|---|
| | | | -20°C -4°F | -10°C +14°F | 0°C 32°F | +10°C +50°F | +20°C +68°F |
| 4300 ➊ | ➋ 81 | Sea Level | 1730 | 1820 | 1920 | 202 ➍ 0 | 0 |
| | | 1000 | 1830 | 1940 | 2040 | 215 | 2290 |
| | | 2000 | 1950 | 2060 | 2170 | 2290 | 2410 |
| | ➌ | | 2070 | 2190 | 2310 | 2440 | |
| | | | 2210 | 2340 | 2470 | 2610 | ➎ |
| | | 5000 | 2360 | 2500 | 2640 | 2790 | 2950 |
| | | 6000 | 2520 | 2680 | 2830 | 2990 | 3160 |
| | | 7000 | 2710 | 2870 | 3040 | 3220 | 3410 |
| | | 8000 | 2910 | 3090 | 3280 | 3470 | 3680 |
| | | 9000 | 3140 | 3340 | 3550 | 3760 | 4070 |
| | | 10,000 | 3390 | 3610 | 3830 | 4150 | 4410 |

*Fig. 2-12. Accelerate-Stop Distance Chart*

The following procedure should be used to determine the accelerate-stop distance for a rejected takeoff. The steps correspond to the numbered callouts on the table.

➊ Enter the chart at a weight of 4,300 pounds.

➋ Proceed horizontally to the critical engine failure speed of 81 KIAS.

➌ Move diagonally to the pressure altitude of 2,000 feet.

➍ Move horizontally to the +20°C temperature column.

➎ Read 2,410 feet, the accelerate-stop distance.

A 2,500-foot runway would be considered critical in this instance if the pilot desired optimum safety. It is important to note that the accelerate-stop distance shown by the chart assumes maximum braking on a paved, dry, level runway.

## CLIMB RATE AND SPEED

After liftoff, the obstacle takeoff profile is to maintain the best angle of climb until clearing all obstacles, then lower the nose to let the airspeed increase to the best rate of climb. Most manufacturers recommend maintaining this airspeed until reaching a safe altitude, then making a transition to cruise climb.

The cruise climb is flown at a higher airspeed, which provides better over-the-nose visibility. The cruise climb also provides better engine cooling.

### MULTI-ENGINE CLIMB

Figure 2-13 illustrates a typical two-engine climb chart and the corresponding rate of climb using maximum continuous power with the landing gear and flaps retracted. This chart is based on standard atmospheric conditions; therefore, performance values must be adjusted when conditions vary from standard (item 1). The chart also specifies the best climb speed for various weights. For example, at a weight of 5,000 pounds, the climb should be conducted at 128 m.p.h. indicated airspeed (item 2).

The dashed line on the chart shows the solution to a typical problem based on the following conditions.

Standard altitude ......... 14,000 ft.
Weight.................... 5,000 lbs.
Temperature ................. 19°F

The two-engine rate of climb is found by entering the chart at the standard altitude of 14,000 feet (item 3), then moving horizontally to the weight of 5,000 pounds (item 4). From this point, the line is followed vertically downward to 2,050 feet per minute (item 5), the rate of climb for a standard day at that altitude.

The standard temperature is found by entering the chart at the standard altitude and moving horizontally to the right until intersecting the standard temperature line (item 6). From this point, a line is followed vertically downward to read the standard temperature of nine degrees Fahrenheit (item 7).

The airplane's outside air temperature gauge is compared to the standard tem-

Fig. 2-13. Two-Engine Climb Chart

perature. Since the thermometer reads 19° Fahrenheit, there is a +10° difference. The rate of climb is adjusted to 2,000 f.p.m. after reference to the note (item 1).

### SINGLE-ENGINE CLIMB

The single-engine rate-of-climb chart, shown in figure 2-14, is also unique to multi-engine operations and provides some very important information. This chart is based on using maximum continuous power on the operative engine with the landing gear and flaps retracted while maintaining the specified airspeed (item 1). In addition, the inoperative engine's propeller is feathered rather than windmilling.

The dashed line in figure 2-14 shows the solution to a typical problem using the same conditions outlined for the two-engine climb. The single-engine climb rate is found by entering the chart at

14,000 feet (item 2), then moving horizontally to the gross weight of 5,000 pounds (item 3). From this point a line is followed vertically downward to 380 f.p.m. (item 4), the rate of climb for a standard day at that altitude.

The standard temperature and temperature difference are found in the same manner as the previous two-engine example by using items 5 and 6. In this case, the rate of climb is reduced by 25 f.p.m. to 355 f.p.m. Additional adjustments may be required if the airplane is being flown in other than a clean configuration (item 7).

Two other important figures that can be obtained from this chart or from the listed performance data are the single-engine service ceiling and the single-engine absolute ceiling. The *single-engine service ceiling* is the maximum altitude at which the airplane can produce a 50

ASSOCIATED CONDITIONS:

| | | |
|---|---|---|
| POWER | MAXIMUM CONTINUOUS | |
| FLAPS | UP | |
| GEAR | UP | |
| CLIMB SPEED | IAS AS TABULATED | |
| INOPERATIVE PROPELLER | FEATHERED | |

NOTE: DECREASE RATE-OF-CLIMB 25 FT/MIN FOR EACH
10°F ABOVE STANDARD DAY (ISA) TEMPERATURE.

## SINGLE ENGINE CLIMB
### STANDARD DAY (ISA)

| WEIGHT POUNDS | CLIMB SPEED MPH ~ IAS |
|---|---|
| 5990 | 122 |
| 5500 | 119 |
| 5000 | 116 |
| 4500 | 113 |

| CONFIGURATION | APPROXIMATE RATE-OF-CLIMB LOSS ~ FT/MIN |
|---|---|
| GEAR DOWN | 200 |
| PROP WINDMILLING | 200 |
| GEAR DOWN AND PROP WINDMILLING | 400 |

*Fig. 2-14. Single-Engine Climb Chart*

f.p.m. rate of climb with the critical engine (if appropriate) inoperative.

This service ceiling can be found on the chart by proceeding vertically upward on the 50 f.p.m. rate-of-climb line to the airplane's gross weight line and reading the service ceiling of 23,600 feet (item 8) to the left.

The *single-engine absolute ceiling* is the altitude at which the airplane will no longer climb with one engine inoperative. This important altitude may be determined by moving vertically upward on the zero f.p.m. line to the intersection of the airplane's gross weight line (item 9). At a gross weight of 5,000 pounds, the single-engine absolute ceiling is approximately 24,400 feet.

## CRUISE PERFORMANCE CHARTS

The cruise performance charts in the pilot's operating handbook are used to determine power settings, fuel consumption, true airspeed, and range. It is quite common for more than one of these values to be presented on a single chart, as shown in figure 2-15.

From this chart, the pilot is able to determine the proper engine speed, manifold pressure, fuel flow per engine, and true airspeed. These charts are presented for various power settings such as 45, 55, and 65 percent horsepower. For example, if the airplane is being flown at 65 percent maximum continuous power at 14,000 feet and the outside air temperature is -13° Celsius, the following information can be determined.

Engine speed  . . . . . . . 2,500 r.p.m.
Manifold pressure  . . . . . 30.4 in. Hg
Fuel flow per engine  . . . 18.6 g.p.h.
True airspeed  . . . . . . . . . 200 kts.

### RANGE PROFILE

The range profile chart utilizes pressure altitude and power to determine the true

## CRUISE POWER SETTINGS

65% MAXIMUM CONTINUOUS POWER (OR FULL THROTTLE)

| PRESS ALT. | ISA-36°F (-20°C) | | | | | | | STANDARD DAY (ISA) | | | | | | | ISA +36°F (+20°C) | | | | | | |
|---|---|---|---|---|---|---|---|---|---|---|---|---|---|---|---|---|---|---|---|---|---|
| | OAT | ENGINE SPEED | MAN. PRESS | FUEL FLOW PER ENGINE | | TAS | | OAT | ENGINE SPEED | MAN. PRESS | FUEL FLOW PER ENGINE | | TAS | | OAT | ENGINE SPEED | MAN PRESS | FUEL FLOW PER ENGINE | | TAS | |
| FEET | °C | RPM | IN HG | PPH | GPH | KTS | MPH | °C | RPM | IN HG | PPH | GPH | KTS | MPH | °C | RPM | IN HG | PPH | GPH | KTS | MPH |
| SL | -5 | 2500 | 28.9 | 112 | 18.6 | 173 | 199 | 15 | 2500 | 29.8 | 112 | 18.6 | 177 | 204 | 35 | 2500 | 30.6 | 112 | 18.6 | 180 | 207 |
| 2000 | -9 | 2500 | 28.9 | 112 | 18.6 | 176 | 203 | 11 | 2500 | 29.8 | 112 | 18.6 | 180 | 207 | 31 | 2500 | 30.7 | 112 | 18.6 | 183 | 211 |
| 4000 | -13 | 2500 | 29.0 | 112 | 18.6 | 179 | 206 | 7 | 2500 | 29.8 | 112 | 18.6 | 183 | 211 | 27 | 2500 | 30.9 | 112 | 18.6 | 186 | 214 |
| 6000 | -17 | 2500 | 29.0 | 112 | 18.6 | 182 | 209 | 3 | 2500 | 29.9 | 112 | 18.6 | 186 | 214 | 23 | 2500 | 31.0 | 112 | 18.6 | 190 | 219 |
| 8000 | -21 | 2500 | 29.2 | 112 | 18.6 | 185 | 213 | -1 | 2500 | 30.0 | 112 | 18.6 | 189 | 218 | 19 | 2500 | 31.1 | 112 | 18.6 | 193 | 222 |
| 10000 | -25 | 2500 | 29.2 | 112 | 18.6 | 188 | 216 | -5 | 2500 | 30.2 | 112 | 18.6 | 193 | 222 | 15 | 2500 | 31.2 | 112 | 18.6 | 197 | 227 |
| 12000 | -29 | 2500 | 29.2 | 112 | 18.6 | 192 | | -9 | 2500 | 30.3 | 112 | 18.6 | 196 | 226 | 11 | 2500 | 31.4 | 112 | 18.6 | 200 | 230 |
| 14000 | -33 | 2500 | 29.2 | 112 | 18.6 | 195 | 224 | -13 | 2500 | 30.4 | 112 | 18.6 | 200 | 230 | 7 | 2500 | 31.5 | 112 | 18.6 | 204 | 235 |
| 16000 | -37 | 2500 | 29.3 | 112 | 18.6 | 199 | 229 | -17 | 2500 | 30.5 | 112 | 18.6 | 204 | 235 | 3 | 2500 | 31.6 | 112 | 18.6 | 208 | 239 |
| 18000 | -41 | 2500 | 29.3 | 112 | 18.6 | 202 | 233 | -21 | 2500 | 30.6 | 112 | 18.6 | 207 | 238 | -1 | 2500 | 31.7 | 112 | 18.6 | 212 | 244 |
| 20000 | -44 | 2500 | 29.4 | 112 | 18.6 | 206 | 237 | -24 | 2500 | 30.6 | 112 | 18.6 | 211 | 243 | -4 | 2500 | 31.8 | 112 | 18.6 | 216 | 249 |
| 22000 | -48 | 2500 | 29.5 | 112 | 18.6 | 211 | 243 | -28 | 2500 | 30.8 | 112 | 18.6 | 216 | 249 | -8 | 2500 | 32.0 | 112 | 18.6 | 221 | 254 |
| 24000 | -53 | 2500 | 29.8 | 112 | 18.6 | 215 | 247 | -33 | 2500 | 31.1 | 112 | 18.6 | 220 | 253 | -13 | 2500 | 32.0 | 111 | 18.5 | 224 | 258 |
| 26000 | -57 | 2500 | 30.0 | 112 | 18.6 | 219 | 252 | -37 | 2500 | 31.3 | 112 | 18.6 | 225 | 259 | -17 | 2500 | 32.0 | 109 | 18.2 | 227 | 261 |
| 28000 | -61 | 2500 | 29.9 | 110 | 18.3 | 222 | 256 | -41 | 2500 | 29.9 | 105 | 17.5 | 223 | 257 | -21 | 2500 | 29.9 | 100 | 16.7 | 223 | 257 |
| 30000 | -64 | 2500 | 26.4 | 94 | 15.7 | 210 | 242 | -44 | 2500 | 26.4 | 91 | 15.1 | 210 | 242 | -24 | 2500 | 26.4 | 88 | 14.7 | 206 | 237 |

NOTES: 1. FULL THROTTLE MANIFOLD PRESSURE SETTINGS ARE APPROXIMATE.
2. ACTUAL BRAKE HORSEPOWER FOR FULL THROTTLE CONDITIONS (ABOVE CRITICAL ALTITUDE) MAY BE DETERMINED BY ENTERING THE GRAPH OF FUEL FLOW VS. BRAKE HORSEPOWER AT THE APPROPRIATE FUEL FLOW.
3. SHADED AREA REPRESENTS OPERATION WITH FULL THROTTLE.

*Fig. 2-15. Cruise Power Settings*

airspeed and range in nautical miles. The chart in figure 2-16 provides the range available with three different fuel tank configurations. This chart will be used to determine approximate KTAS and range in nautical miles under the following conditions.

Pressure altitude . . . . . . 10,000 ft.
Brake horsepower . . . . . . . . . . . .65%
Fuel . . . . . . . . . . . . . . . 978 lbs.

The chart is entered from the left margin at pressure altitude of 10,000 (item 1). A line is followed horizontally until it reaches the diagonal 65 percent BHP line (item 2). The appropriate true airspeed is read at this intersection. The approximate no-wind range of 970 n.m. (item 3) is read at the bottom of the chart on the scale for a 978-pound fuel load.

This particular range profile chart's information includes fuel required for start, taxi, takeoff, cruise climb to altitude, cruise, descent and 45 minutes reserve fuel at 45 percent power. The distances shown are the sum of the distances to climb, cruise, and descend.

## NORMAL LANDING DISTANCE CHARTS

Charts also are supplied to determine the distance required to stop after landing. The normal landing distance chart presented in figure 2-17 provides landing information for a normal ground roll and the total distance to clear a 50-foot obstacle using different landing gross weights, speeds, pressure altitudes, and temperatures.

Under the listed conditions, the expected landing ground roll and total distance to clear a 50-foot obstacle are 500 feet and 1,650 feet, respectively.

Weight . . . . . . . . . . . . . . . . . . . .4,600 lbs.
Speed at obstacle . . . . . . . . . 86 KIAS

## RANGE PROFILE

CONDITIONS:
1. Starting Weight - 5500 Pounds.
2. Cruise Climb to Desired Altitude.
3. Recommended Lean Fuel Flow.
4. Zero Wind.
5. Standard Day.

NOTE:
1. Range computations include fuel required for start, taxi, takeoff, cruise climb to altitude, cruise, descent and 45 minutes holding fuel at 45% power.
2. The distances shown are the sum of the distances to climb, cruise and descend.

*Fig. 2-16. Range Profile Chart*

Temperature ................. 20°C
Pressure altitude .......... 2,000 ft.

The specified conditions of a hard-surfaced, level, dry runway, 35° flaps, and maximum braking effort are also included. Since different runway conditions require certain adjustments, various allowances are included in the note section.

## STALLING SPEED CHARTS

Power-off stalling speeds vary with different flap settings, weights, and bank angles. The power-off stalling speeds appropriate to these factors can be determined from the stalling speed versus weight and stalling speed versus angle-of-bank charts.

# NORMAL LANDING DISTANCE

CONDITIONS:
1. Throttles - IDLE.
2. Landing Gear - DOWN.
3. Wing Flaps - 35°.
4. Cowl Flaps - CLOSE.
5. Level, Hard Surface Runway.
6. Maximum Braking Effort.

NOTE:
1. Increase distance by 25% of ground run for operation on firm sod runway.
2. If necessary to land with wing flaps UP, the approach speed should be increased above the normal approach speed by 12 knots. Expect total landing distance to increase by 35%.
3. Decrease total distances by 3% for each 4 knots headwind. For operations with tailwinds up to 10 knots, increase total distances by 5% for each 2 knots wind.

| WEIGHT-POUNDS | SPEED AT 50-FOOT OBSTACLE KIAS | PRESSURE ALTITUDE - FEET | 20°C (68°F) | | 30°C (86°F) | | 40°C (104°F) | |
|---|---|---|---|---|---|---|---|---|
| | | | GROUND ROLL - FEET | TOTAL DISTANCE TO CLEAR 50-FOOT OBSTACLE | GROUND ROLL - FEET | TOTAL DISTANCE TO CLEAR 50-FOOT OBSTACLE | GROUND ROLL - FEET | TOTAL DISTANCE TO CLEAR 50-FOOT OBSTACLE |
| 5400 | 93 | Sea Level | 660 | 1810 | 680 | 1830 | 700 | 1850 |
| | | 1000 | 680 | 1830 | 700 | 1850 | 730 | 1880 |
| | | 2000 | 710 | 1860 | 730 | 1880 | 750 | 1900 |
| | | 3000 | 730 | 1880 | 760 | 1910 | 780 | 1930 |
| | | 4000 | 760 | 1910 | 780 | 1930 | 810 | 1960 |
| | | 5000 | 790 | 1940 | 810 | 1960 | 840 | 1990 |
| | | 6000 | 820 | 1970 | 850 | 2000 | 870 | 2020 |
| | | 7000 | 850 | 2000 | 880 | 2030 | 910 | 2060 |
| | | 8000 | 880 | 2030 | 910 | 2060 | 940 | 2090 |
| | | 9000 | 920 | 2070 | 950 | 2100 | 980 | 2130 |
| | | 10,000 | 950 | 2100 | 980 | 2130 | 1020 | 2170 |
| 5000 | 89 | Sea Level | 550 | 1700 | 570 | 1720 | 590 | 1740 |
| | | 1000 | 570 | 1720 | 590 | 1740 | 610 | 1760 |
| | | 2000 | 600 | 1750 | 620 | 1770 | 640 | 1790 |
| | | 3000 | 620 | 1770 | 640 | 1790 | 660 | 1810 |
| | | 4000 | 640 | 1790 | 660 | 1810 | 680 | 1830 |
| | | 5000 | 670 | 1820 | 690 | 1840 | 710 | 1860 |
| | | 6000 | 690 | 1840 | 710 | 1860 | 740 | 1890 |
| | | 7000 | 720 | 1870 | 740 | 1890 | 770 | 1920 |
| | | 8000 | 750 | 1900 | 770 | 1920 | 800 | 1950 |
| | | 9000 | 770 | 1920 | 800 | 1950 | 830 | 1980 |
| | | 10,000 | 800 | 1950 | 830 | 1980 | 860 | 2010 |
| 4600 | 86 | Sea Level | 460 | 1610 | 480 | 1630 | 490 | 1640 |
| | | 1000 | 480 | 1630 | 500 | 1650 | 510 | 1660 |
| | | 2000 | 500 | 1650 | 510 | 1660 | 530 | 1680 |
| | | 3000 | 520 | 1670 | 530 | 1680 | 550 | 1700 |
| | | 4000 | 530 | 1680 | 550 | 1700 | 570 | 1720 |
| | | 5000 | 550 | 1700 | 570 | 1720 | 590 | 1740 |
| | | 6000 | 580 | 1730 | 600 | 1750 | 610 | 1760 |
| | | 7000 | 600 | 1750 | 620 | 1770 | 640 | 1790 |
| | | 8000 | 620 | 1770 | 640 | 1790 | 660 | 1810 |
| | | 9000 | 650 | 1800 | 670 | 1820 | 690 | 1840 |
| | | 10,000 | 670 | 1820 | 690 | 1840 | 720 | 1870 |
| 4200 | 82 | Sea Level | 380 | 1530 | 390 | 1540 | 410 | 1560 |
| | | 1000 | 390 | 1540 | 410 | 1560 | 420 | 1570 |
| | | 2000 | 410 | 1560 | 420 | 1570 | 440 | 1590 |
| | | 3000 | 420 | 1570 | 440 | 1590 | 450 | 1600 |
| | | 4000 | 440 | 1590 | 450 | 1600 | 470 | 1620 |
| | | 5000 | 460 | 1610 | 470 | 1620 | 490 | 1640 |
| | | 6000 | 470 | 1620 | 490 | 1640 | 500 | 1650 |
| | | 7000 | 490 | 1640 | 510 | 1660 | 520 | 1670 |
| | | 8000 | 510 | 1660 | 530 | 1680 | 540 | 1690 |
| | | 9000 | 530 | 1680 | 550 | 1700 | 560 | 1710 |
| | | 10,000 | 550 | 1700 | 570 | 1720 | 590 | 1740 |

*Fig. 2-17. Normal Landing Distance Chart*

## WEIGHT

Figure 2-18 shows the power-off, level flight stalling speed at various weights with the gear extended. The upper line represents the stalling speed with the flaps retracted. Since the stalling speed on the chart is given in calibrated airspeed, the pilot must use the airspeed correction table to determine the appropriate indicated airspeed.

The dashed lines in figure 2-18 represent the solution to a typical problem under the following conditions.

Power ......................... Off
Weight.................... 4,200 lbs.
Landing gear ........... Extended

The appropriate stalling speed with flaps retracted is 76 m.p.h. CAS (item 1).

Fig. 2-18. Stalling Speed vs. Weight

Fig. 2-19. Stalling Speed vs. Angle of Bank

Extension of 40° of flaps decreases the stalling speed to about 69 m.p.h. CAS (item 2).

### ANGLE OF BANK

Figure 2-19 illustrates the stalling speeds with the gear extended at various angles of bank. The top line represents an airplane with the flaps retracted and the lower line represents one with the flaps extended. The dashed lines represent the solution to a problem under the listed conditions.

Power ................. Off
Gross weight ........ 4,200 lbs.
Gear ............. Extended

The appropriate stalling speed with flaps retracted is approximately 92 m.p.h. CAS (item 1). Extension of 40° of flaps decreases the stalling speed to about 83 m.p.h. CAS (item 2).

# chapter 3

# INTRODUCTION

The failure of an engine leaves the multi-engine pilot with more alternatives than the single-engine airplane pilot. However, the exact parameters of those alternatives are more difficult to define. This chapter provides a framework for determining the performance that can be expected following an engine failure and explains the aerodynamic factors and piloting techniques involved with single-engine flight.

# SECTION A—AERODYNAMICS

When an engine fails, the greatest overall performance loss results from a 50 percent reduction in available horsepower. However, the total loss of *climb performance* when one engine fails is approximately 80 percent for most light, conventional, twin-engine airplanes. Since climb performance is based on excess power available, an engine failure reduces excess power by more than one-half because of the sharp increase in drag that the remaining engine's power must overcome. The sudden drag increase results from asymmetrical thrust and the control responses needed to counter yawing and rolling tendencies. This means a multi-engine airplane may not climb at all with one engine inoperative. Although aircraft certified under FAR Part 23 are required to meet certain performance and handling criteria, many light twin-engine airplanes are not required to demonstrate climbing ability during single-engine operations. The regulation requires a positive engine-out rate of climb at 5,000 feet density altitude only for those multi-engine airplanes weighing more than 6,000 pounds and/or having a stalling speed ($V_{SO}$) greater than 61 knots. If the airplane weighs 6,000 pounds or less and has a stalling speed of 61 knots or less, a specific, *positive* engine-out rate of climb is not required. However, the manufacturer must determine what the engine-out climb performance is at 5,000 feet with the critical engine inoperative and its propeller in the minimum drag configuration.

## CRITICAL ENGINE

The term *critical engine* refers to the engine whose failure most adversely affects the performance or handling characteristics of the airplane. Consideration of the critical engine is most significant in situations where the airplane is operating at low speeds with a high power setting. In these high angle of attack attitudes, the descending blade of each propeller is producing more thrust than the ascending blade. The unequal thrust vector can be related to the "moment" presented in weight and balance. The longitudinal axis of the airplane is considered the datum for this discussion, and each of the descending propeller blades is given an "arm." Thus, the thrust from each engine may be measured as a "moment arm," as illustrated in figure 3-1.

*Fig. 3-1. Critical Engine*

If the left engine failed, directional control would be affected more than if the right engine became inoperative. The larger moment arm associated with the right engine would have a greater influence than that of the left engine, as shown in figure 3-2. Therefore, in conventional multi-engine airplanes without counterrotating engines, the left engine is critical.

## MINIMUM CONTROL SPEED

Each multi-engine airplane certified under FAR Part 23 has an established minimum control speed ($V_{MC}$) with the critical engine inoperative and the other engine developing takeoff power. $V_{MC}$ is established under specified criteria including conditions that affect controllability. The propeller of the failed engine is windmilling, or feathered if equipped with an automatic feathering device. The wing and cowl flaps are in the takeoff position, and the landing gear is retracted. The airplane is loaded to maximum takeoff weight (or any lesser weight necessary to show $V_{MC}$) with the most unfavorable center of gravity. Finally, a bank angle of not more than five degrees is established toward the good engine.

The established $V_{MC}$ is found in the pilot's operating handbook and is normally shown on the airspeed indicator with a red radial line. However, the actual $V_{MC}$ varies as any of the specified conditions change. For example, data obtained from full-scale wind tunnel tests of a light twin aircraft show that aircraft weight directly affects $V_{MC}$. The tests show that as weight decreases, actual $V_{MC}$ increases. The wind tunnel tests also confirm that as the CG shifts forward, $V_{MC}$ decreases. In this case, the rudder is more effective in counteracting the yawing tendency due to the longer arm through which it works. Another variable is the power output of the operating engine. If power is decreased, the tendency for the airplane to yaw and roll toward the inoperative engine is also decreased, lowering $V_{MC}$. Figure 3-3 illustrates that there is a wide range of actual minimum control airspeeds with different power settings. In addition, as altitude increases, normally aspirated engines lose efficiency and are unable to develop 100 percent rated sea level power. This power loss also causes actual $V_{MC}$ to decrease.

While actual $V_{MC}$ is decreasing with altitude, the pilot must remember that the calibrated stalling speed remains the same. Figure 3-4 illustrates the effect of altitude on actual $V_{MC}$ and shows that stalling speed and $V_{MC}$ eventually converge. Therefore, the pilot should not assume that flight below published $V_{MC}$ is safe, even while flying at a high density altitude.

*Fig. 3-2. Engine Failure and Turning Tendencies*

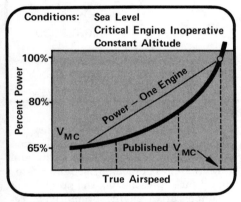

*Fig. 3-3. Percent Power and Minimum Control Speed*

*Fig. 3-4. Effect of Altitude on $V_{MC}$*

## STABILITY AND CONTROL

The primary concern after engine failure is to keep the aircraft controllable and stabilize the attitude for the best performance. Maintaining $V_{MC}$ does not guarantee that the airplane can climb or even hold altitude, but only that the pilot can maintain a heading. Control effectiveness in any flight situation depends on the velocity of the airflow over the control surfaces. At airspeeds below $V_{MC}$, full control deflection does not provide sufficient force to overcome the yawing and rolling tendencies induced by failure of the critical engine.

## IN-FLIGHT FORCES

During flight with one engine inoperative in a multi-engine airplane, the four forces take on new dimensions. Three of them (lift, thrust, and drag) now act on the aircraft asymmetrically, while the management of the fourth (weight) is more critical.

When either engine fails, the induced airflow from the propeller slipstream is lost and total lift on that wing is decreased (excluding airplanes with a centerline thrust configuration). However, the induced airflow from the operating engine is still producing additional lift,

*Fig. 3-5. Asymmetrical Forces*

and this lift differential causes a rolling tendency toward the inoperative engine as shown in figure 3-5, Part A.

Figure 3-5 also illustrates the yawing tendency toward the inoperative engine caused by the asymmetrical thrust condition. This situation causes some of the airflow to be blocked by the fuselage since the flight path is no longer parallel to the longitudinal axis.

When control surfaces, such as the ailerons or the rudder, are displaced from the neutral position, a proportional amount of drag is created. Figure 3-5, Part B illustrates this induced drag as well as the parasite drag created by the propeller of the inoperative engine. Depending on the blade angle, the drag of a windmilling propeller may be as severe as that of a flat disc of the same diameter. Figure 3-6 shows the relation-

ship of the windmilling propeller and stationary propeller to blade angle and drag created. This comparison illustrates importance of feathering the propeller of the inoperative engine promptly to reduce drag, assuming it cannot be restarted immediately.

Situations should be avoided where aircraft loading could affect engine-out operations. As stated earlier, the CG position affects controllability, and loading the airplane to the aft limit increases $V_{MC}$. In airplanes equipped with wing-mounted tanks outboard of the engines, fuel management may also be critical. For example, a heavy fuel load on the side of the critical engine and a light fuel load on the other side should be avoided. As always, loading should follow the recommendations in the pilot's operating handbook.

| PART A | WINGS LEVEL | PART B | BANK TOWARD OPERATING ENGINE (LEFT) |

*Fig. 3-7. Zero Sideslip*

## CONTROL APPLICATION

Considerable control pressures are necessary to counter the rolling and yawing moments encountered during flight with one engine. However, rudder deflection can be minimized if the airplane is banked three to five degrees toward the operative engine. In this configuration, the high wing produces a lift vector which acts to relieve the rudder forces required to maintain straight flight. A common misconception in engine-out operations is that the airplane should be flown with the wings level and the ball centered in the inclinometer, as shown in figure 3-7, part A. This causes a side slip into the inoperative engine as evidenced by the position of the yaw string. Flight tests have shown that this can increase actual $V_{MC}$ by 20 knots in some airplanes and decrease single-engine climb performance by several hundred feet per minute. Banking toward the operative engine reduces $V_{MC}$ and ensures that stall characteristics will not be degraded. Using enough rudder to maintain straight flight while in a three to five degree bank puts the airplane in a zero side slip condition. The ball will be approximately one ball width toward the "good" side, as shown in figure 3-7, Part B.

### COUNTERROTATING ENGINES

When an airplane is equipped with counterrotating propellers, neither engine is considered critical. As illustrated in figure 3-8, asymmetrical thrust is equal,

*Fig. 3-6. Propeller Drag Contribution*

*Fig. 3-8. Asymmetrical Loading with Counterrotating Engines*

regardless of which engine is inoperative. Turning tendencies are still very apparent, but lack the severity of those associated with the critical engine failure of a conventional twin.

## ENGINE-OUT V-SPEEDS

An engine failure in a twin usually means that the best climb performance available is only marginal when compared to the performance with both engines operating. Climb airspeeds are published by the manufacturer for best rate and best angle during single-engine operation. These airspeeds are referred to as $V_{YSE}$ and $V_{XSE}$, respectively. In addition, some manufacturers establish a minimum speed for intentionally rendering one engine inoperative. This speed, which is applicable to training activities, is generally called $V_{SSE}$.

### BEST RATE OF CLIMB—SINGLE ENGINE

$V_{YSE}$ is the speed which produces the greatest gain in altitude in a given amount of time with one engine inoperative. This airspeed normally is used if altitude is a prime consideration after engine failure. If engine failure occurs above the airplane's single-engine service ceiling, this airspeed produces the minimum descent rate with the operative engine at maximum continuous power.

### BEST ANGLE OF CLIMB—SINGLE ENGINE

$V_{XSE}$ is the engine-out best angle-of-climb airspeed. This speed is used for obstruction clearance with one engine inoperative. In most cases, $V_{XSE}$ is a somewhat higher airspeed than the twin-engine best angle-of-climb speed ($V_X$).

## SINGLE-ENGINE CEILINGS

The operating altitudes of multi-engine airplanes are lowered considerably during single-engine flight. The engine loss reduces total thrust available and corresponding reductions of *service ceiling* and *absolute ceiling* result.

### SINGLE-ENGINE SERVICE CEILING

The single-engine service ceiling is the maximum density altitude at which the single-engine best rate-of-climb airspeed ($V_{YSE}$) will produce a 50 f.p.m. rate of climb. The ability to climb 50 f.p.m. in calm air is necessary to maintain *level flight* for long periods in turbulent air. This ceiling assumes the airplane is at gross weight in the clean configuration, the critical engine (if appropriate) inoperative, and the propeller feathered. In comparison, the multi-engine service ceiling is the density altitude at which the best rate-of-climb airspeed ($V_Y$) will produce a 100 f.p.m. rate of climb at gross weight in the clean configuration.

### SINGLE-ENGINE ABSOLUTE CEILING

The single-engine absolute ceiling is the maximum density altitude the airplane is capable of attaining or maintaining. This ceiling assumes the airplane is at gross weight in the clean configuration, the critical engine (if appropriate) inoperative, and the propeller feathered. This is also the density altitude at which $V_{XSE}$ and $V_{YSE}$ are the same airspeed.

Figure 3-9 illustrates an engine failure at a cruising altitude above the single-

*Fig. 3-9. Altitude Loss During Single-Engine Operation*

engine absolute ceiling. In this situation, the aircraft will descend gradually (drift down) to the density altitude equivalent of the single-engine absolute ceiling appropriate to the existing gross weight. In turbulent air, the airplane may not be capable of maintaining the single-engine absolute ceiling and may continue to descend to the single-engine service ceiling or lower.

## SINGLE-ENGINE CLIMB

Climb performance is dependent upon the ratio of thrust to drag. If drag exceeds thrust, climb is not possible and the best rate-of-climb speed will provide the least rate of descent. Figure 3-10 depicts a typical drag curve with available thrust when one engine is inoperative. Any thrust and airspeed combination that falls within the shaded area represents a positive rate of climb. Conversely, any point outside the shaded area will produce a descent. This graph also illustrates the thrust available on the same airplane at 15,000 feet. At that altitude, drag exceeds thrust and a positive rate of climb cannot be established.

Drag is a major factor in the amount of excess thrust available. Any increase in drag, whether parasite or induced, must be balanced by the use of additional thrust. Any use of excess thrust to counteract drag is thrust which cannot be used for the climb. Since the extension of the landing gear and/or flaps increases parasite drag, the maximum amount of excess thrust is available in the clean configuration. In most light and medium twin-engine airplanes, the extension of the landing gear or flaps may increase drag in excess of the available thrust causing a descent.

*Fig. 3-10. Thrust Available for Climb*

Drag also increases because of the rudder and aileron deflections necessary to maintain straight flight and the airflow restriction caused by the inoperative engine's propeller. An increase in airspeed also increases drag. Therefore, any speed above that necessary to maintain level flight or above $V_{YSE}$ during a climb requires excess thrust and decreases the airplane's performance. All of this results in a dramatic decrease in performance.

It is important that the pilot be familiar with the correct order for drag reduction following an engine failure. Normally, a windmilling propeller contributes the greatest amount of drag, followed by full flaps, extended landing gear, and the control deflections required to stop the airplane from turning. Since it is considered unwise to immediately feather an engine before it has been positively identified, drag is normally reduced by first retracting flaps and gear. Next, the failed engine is identified and the propeller is feathered. However, the specific order of drag reduction may vary between types of twin-engine airplanes, so the manufacturer's recommendations should be followed. During training, it is beneficial to use the vertical velocity indicator to compare the relative engine-out performance loss associated with a windmilling propeller, full flaps, and extended landing gear.

Performance will be decreased still further by any increase in density altitude. Density altitude will affect the single-engine climb rate as it affects the twin-engine climb rate, but the results are more critical during engine-out operations. For example, the single-engine climb rate normally is very small for most light multi-engine airplanes. Therefore, any decrease in this performance because of higher density altitude will quickly result in a negligible climb rate or a possible descent.

The climb performance can be improved greatly by reducing operating gross weights. As an example, a typical multi-engine airplane's sea level single-engine climb rate may increase from 230 f.p.m. at 4,000 pounds gross weight to 420 f.p.m. at 3,400 pounds. At the same time, the single-engine service ceiling may increase from 5,200 feet to 10,000 feet under standard atmospheric conditions.

With regard to the above performance considerations, it is evident that the takeoff and climb are the most critical phases of all multi-engine operations. During this time, the airplane is the heaviest it will be throughout the flight. Therefore, the single-engine rate of climb and service ceiling are the lowest.

Turns, except to avoid obstructions, should be limited during a single-engine climb until the airplane has reached a safe altitude to return to the airport. Even a perfectly coordinated turn increases induced drag which, in turn, increases the amount of thrust required to maintain altitude. This results in less excess thrust for climb. If a turn is necessary, the smallest bank angle possible for the existing conditions should be used. To illustrate this point, figure 3-11 shows that, at a constant airspeed, a 15° bank increases the induced drag by approximately seven percent while a 30° bank results in a 33 percent increase.

Because of the increased drag and decreased control effectiveness, it is recommended that the maximum bank angle of 15° be used during single-engine maneuvering and then only after a safe maneuvering altitude is attained. The 15° bank should be maximum because of the rapid drag increase associated with higher bank angles. As illustrated, a five degree increase from 15° to 20° of bank nearly doubles the percentage increase in induced drag.

| BANK ANGLE, DEGREES | LOAD FACTOR | PERCENT INCREASE IN STALL SPEED | PERCENT INCREASE IN INDUCED DRAG (AT CONSTANT VELOCITY) |
|---|---|---|---|
| 0 . . . . . . . . | 1.0000 | 0 | 0 |
| 5 . . . . . . . . | 1.0038 | 0.2 | 0.8 |
| 10 . . . . . . . . | 1.0154 | 0.7 | 3.1 |
| 15 . . . . . . . . | 1.0353 | 1.7 | 7.2 |
| 20 . . . . . . . . | 1.0642 | 3.2 | 13.3 |
| 25 . . . . . . . . | 1.1034 | 5.0 | 21.7 |
| 30 . . . . . . . . | 1.1547 | 7.5 | 33.3 |
| 35 . . . . . . . . | 1.2208 | 10.5 | 49.0 |
| 40 . . . . . . . . | 1.3054 | 14.3 | 70.4 |
| 45 . . . . . . . . | 1.4142 | 18.9 | 100.0 |
| 60 . . . . . . . . | 2.0000 | 41.4 | 300.0 |

*Fig. 3-11. Bank Angle and Induced Drag*

The entire discussion of asymmetrical thrust, $V_{MC}$, and single-engine climbs has pointed out that takeoff and initial climb are the most critical phases of multi-engine operations. The pilot must continually analyze his aircraft's performance in order to know what single-engine performance can be expected in the event of engine failure or partial power loss.

# SECTION B—PROCEDURES AND MANEUVERS

As discussed in the previous section, the aerodynamic factors affecting flight with one engine inoperative are significant and critical. This section will apply these aerodynamic relationships to the practical aspects of engine-out operations, beginning with engine shutdown procedures and followed by in-flight maneuvers.

## ENGINE SHUTDOWN

The decision to shut down a failing engine is a matter of pilot judgment, based on the circumstances involved at that particular time. If an engine has failed completely, it is obvious that it should be shut down and the propeller feathered to reduce drag. However, the pilot should seriously consider continued use of an engine that is producing partial power. Even though maximum power is not available, a reduced power output is better than none.

### IDENTIFYING THE INOPERATIVE ENGINE

After an engine has failed, the pilot's primary concern is to maintain control of the airplane and identify the inoperative engine. The following discussion pertains to the techniques of identifying the failed engine. Actual shutdown procedures will be discussed later in this chapter.

#### YAW AND ROLL

The first indication of an engine failure is a pronounced yaw and roll, which always occurs in the direction of the inoperative engine. As these conditions develop, the pilot must apply rudder to maintain a constant heading. The control application provides a second indication of the inoperative engine because the foot which is not applying rudder pressure is on the same side as the failed engine. The memory aid, "idle foot, idle engine," often is used in multi-engine

training to identify a failed engine. For example, if the airplane begins to yaw to the right, the pilot must apply left rudder to maintain directional control. Therefore, his right foot is not applying rudder pressure, which corresponds to the failed right engine.

#### ENGINE INSTRUMENTS

Certain engine instruments also may aid the pilot in identifying the failed engine. Specifically, the fuel-flow and fuel-pressure gauges should be observed to determine if the failure was caused by fuel starvation. In addition, the EGT and cylinder head temperatures may be decreasing or lower than those of the operating engine. Figure 3-12 lists important indications of a failed engine.

1. **PRONOUNCED YAWING AND ROLLING TENDENCY**
2. **HEAVY RUDDER PRESSURE REQUIRED FOR DIRECTIONAL CONTROL**
3. **LOSS IN FUEL FLOW ON ONE ENGINE**
4. **COOLER CYLINDER HEAD TEMPERATURE ON ONE ENGINE**

*Fig. 3-12. Indications of a Failed Engine*

#### ENGINE POWER CONTROLS

At the same time the pilot is regaining control of the airplane and checking the engine instruments, the mixtures are advanced to *full rich*, the propellers are moved to *high r.p.m.*, and the throttles are advanced to *maximum power*. This procedure guarantees that the operating engine is producing maximum power, regardless of which engine is inoperative. During this application of power, special attention must be given to directional control, because as the power is increased, the amount of required rudder also will increase. In addition, as directional control is maintained, the airspeed must remain at best rate-of-climb airspeed ($V_{YSE}$).

### VERIFICATION

After the inoperative engine has been identified, it is vital to *verify* that the correct analysis has been made. To verify the inoperative engine and safeguard against shutting down the operating engine, the pilot should retard the throttle on the *suspected* failed engine. If the correct engine has been selected there will be no change in airplane performance or the amount of rudder pressure required to counteract yaw. If the engine is developing partial power, the yawing tendency will increase as the throttle is retarded. In this case, it may be desirable to keep the engine operating until a safe altitude is reached and the nature of the problem determined. However, if the incorrect engine has been selected, the

yawing tendency will decrease, and the throttle must be advanced immediately to regain maximum engine power. Failure to first identify and then verify the failed engine before shutdown can have grave consequences, as depicted in figure 3-13.

## ENGINE SHUTDOWN PROCEDURES

Since the engine shutdown and securing procedures may vary between each make and model of airplane, the appropriate pilot's operating handbook should be consulted for specific details. However, the basic procedures are similar for all piston engine airplanes. The expanded list of steps shown in figure 3-14 is a typical checklist.

Items 1 through 11 should be committed to memory so they are available for immediate recall and action in the event of an engine failure. If time permits after the airplane is trimmed, the pilot should complete the entire printed engine-out checklist to verify all items have been completed. In addition, during this re-

Fig. 3-13. Failing to Verify the Failed Engine

## ENGINE SHUTDOWN AND SECURING PROCEDURES

1. Maintain directional control by applying rudder to maintain a constant heading.
2. Maintain $V_{YSE}$ as a minimum airspeed.
3. Apply maximum power by moving the mixtures, props, and throttles full forward.
4. Reduce the drag by retracting the flaps and landing gear.
5. Check auxiliary fuel boost pumps—ON.
6. Check that the fuel selector is in the proper position.
7. Identify the inoperative engine by using the "idle foot, idle engine" test.
8. Verify the inoperative engine by closing the appropriate throttle.
9. Feather the propeller by moving the propeller lever to the feather position.
10. Move the mixture control to idle cutoff.
11. Trim excess control pressures.
12. Secure the inoperative engine by using the following steps.
    A. Fuel selector—OFF
    B. Auxiliary boost pump—OFF
    C. Magneto switches—OFF
    D. Alternator—OFF
    E. Cowl Flap—CLOSED
13. Review checklist.

*Fig. 3-14. Engine Shutdown Checklist*

view, the inoperative engine should be secured and the prelanding checklist reviewed.

If the engine failure occurs during the takeoff or initial climb, it is obvious that single-engine performance is at its most critical level. In this condition, the maintenance of $V_{YSE}$ (or $V_{XSE}$ if obstacles are a factor), prompt identification of the inoperative engine, and propeller feathering are of prime importance. If the pretakeoff checklist has been followed correctly, the pilot can be sure that the fuel selectors are on the proper tanks, the boost pumps are on, the propeller controls are full forward, and the mixtures are set properly. Therefore, if the engine failure occurs on takeoff, only a quick review of these items is necessary prior to engine identification and propeller feathering. In this manner, optimum single-engine performance may be achieved in a minimum amount of time.

If an engine failure occurs during cruise, a prompt engine shutdown is not as

critical. In this situation, the pilot normally has adequate time to analyze the problem and attempt to restore the engine's power. If the problem cannot be remedied, the engine should be shut down and the propeller feathered to conserve altitude.

### ENGINE SHUTDOWN RAMIFICATIONS

In addition to the shutdown of the inoperative engine, the pilot must give close attention to the operating engine from two standpoints. First, the combination of reduced airspeed and additional power demanded from the engine may cause overheating problems. Therefore, the oil temperature, oil pressure, and cylinder head temperature must be monitored and maintained in the normal operating ranges. If necessary, the cowl flaps should be opened and the mixture enriched to aid in engine temperature reduction. Second, single-engine flight also creates single alternator operation, which requires an appropriate reduction in electrical load. In addition, other systems such as hydraulics and pneumatics may have greatly reduced capabilities or become completely inoperative.

## PROPELLER UNFEATHERING AND ENGINE RESTART

A common occurrence during multi-engine flight training is the propeller unfeathering and engine restart procedure. Figure 3-15 shows a typical checklist used for this procedure. It should be noted that item 6 calls for use of the engine starter to begin propeller rotation. This is necessary to create oil pressure from the propeller governor, which begins to move the propeller blades from high pitch (feather) to low pitch. The starter can be disengaged as the blades move out of the feather position, because the airflow passing over the blades will continue the rotation. Once the engine starts, the power should be kept to a minimum until the cylinder head and oil temperatures are within the normal operating ranges. This is important because the use of high power settings on a cold engine can result in engine damage.

## RESTARTING PROCEDURES

1. Magneto Switches—ON
2. Fuel Selector—MAIN TANK
3. Throttle—FORWARD approximately one inch
4. Mixture—AS REQUIRED for flight altitude
5. Propeller—FORWARD of detent
6. Starter Button—PRESS—RELEASE when engine fires
7. Mixture—AS REQUIRED
8. Power—INCREASE after cylinder head temperature is adequate
9. Cowl Flap—AS REQUIRED
10. Alternator—ON

Fig. 3-15. In-Flight Engine Restart Procedure

If an engine is equipped with *unfeathering accumulators*, it is not necessary to use the starter to begin propeller rotation. The accumulator provides either hydraulic or pneumatic pressure to the feathering mechanism, which forces the blades out of the feather position. As the blades move from feather towards low pitch, the propellers gain sufficient blade angle to begin rotation because of the airflow. The propeller accumulator usually is activated by moving the appropriate propeller control lever full forward to the high r.p.m. setting.

## ENGINE-OUT MANEUVERS

As previously discussed, the competent multi-engine pilot should be prepared for an engine failure during all phases of flight. Although the possibilities of an actual engine failure are somewhat remote, the pilot should always have a plan of action in the event of such an occurrence.

### TAKEOFF

If the engine failure occurs during the takeoff ground run, the airplane will immediately turn in the direction of the failed engine. If this condition develops below the single-engine minimum control airspeed, the takeoff *must be discontinued*. In all twin-engine airplanes, this means closing both throttles immediately and applying braking as necessary to stop the airplane.

If the failure occurs when the airplane is airborne and sufficient runway remains for landing, the pilot should close both throttles and land, particularly if the landing gear is still extended. If the landing cannot be accomplished safely, a single-engine climb should be established to a safe maneuvering altitude, followed by a return to the airport for landing.

Under some circumstances, the pilot may elect to take off when the density altitude exceeds the airplane's single-engine service ceiling. When operating within this limitation, the pilot must not expect the airplane to have any single-engine climb capability. If engine failure occurs in this situation, the only alternative available is the prompt selection of a suitable off-airport landing area within the airplane's driftdown range. Under no circumstances can the pilot allow the airspeed to become lower than $V_{MC}$. The single-engine best rate-of-climb ($V_{YSE}$) airspeed should be maintained to provide the slowest rate of descent.

## CLIMB

For normal multi-engine takeoffs, it is important to maintain $V_Y$ during the initial climb. Any airspeed in excess of $V_Y$ is not as valuable as the altitude that would have been gained since the drag of a failed engine will prevent efficient conversion of excess airspeed to altitude. If an engine failure occurs during climb at an airspeed of $V_Y$ (after the landing gear and the flaps are retracted), the possibility of a sustained single-engine climb is greatly improved.

If an engine failure occurs during the climb and there are no obstacles to be cleared, the single-engine best rate-of-climb ($V_{YSE}$) should be maintained at the maximum continuous power setting. If the airspeed is below $V_{YSE}$, a momentary descent will be required to accelerate the airplane to the single-engine best rate-of-climb airspeed before the climb can be initiated. The pilots of light and medium twin-engine airplanes must realize that these airplanes have very narrow single-engine performance parameters. Any airspeed *above* or *below* $V_{YSE}$ results in a reduced rate of climb.

To gain optimum single-engine performance during the climb, the airplane should be banked up to five degrees toward the operating engine. This technique reduces the amount of rudder deflection required to maintain directional control and, therefore, reduces drag. The drag is reduced because the high wing produces addition lift which acts to assist rudder forces in turning the airplane away from the inoperative engine. Figure 3-16 shows that, in the case of

the left engine out (position 1), a lift vector is created to the right because of the raised left wing.

The opposite is true if the airplane is banked toward the inoperative engine (position 2). In this situation, a lift vector is produced in the same direction as the yaw, requiring additional rudder deflection to overcome the turn vector. For this reason, the pilot must use extra care when turning in the direction of the inoperative engine. Turns in this direction can be made safely if the pilot is aware of the aerodynamic forces involved and maintains a safe margin above $V_{MC}$.

## ENROUTE

As a general rule, an engine failure during the enroute phase of flight is not as critical as one which occurs during takeoff or climb. The pilot should have ample time to analyze the reason for the failure, attempt a restart, or secure the engine if it cannot be restarted. Even if the situation is not critical, it is good practice to apply full power to the good engine to conserve altitude during the attempt to correct the engine failure. As with every engine failure, the mixtures should be moved to full rich, the props moved to high r.p.m., the boost pumps turned on, and the fuel tanks checked to be sure the tank in use has fuel. Even if the tank has fuel, it is a good practice to select another tank which has fuel, since the fuel line from the original tank may be blocked. These steps are important because the most frequent cause of an enroute engine failure is fuel starvation.

When single-engine operations become necessary, the original cruising altitude often is higher than the airplane's single-engine absolute or service ceiling. In this situation, the pilot must accept the fact that a descent is inevitable until the airplane reaches the absolute ceiling. During the descent, $V_{YSE}$ airspeed should be used to obtain the minimum

CORRECT PROCEDURE

POSITION 1

INCORRECT PROCEDURE

POSITION 2

*Fig. 3-16. Bank During Engine-Out Operations*

rate of descent and conserve altitude as long as possible. The airspeed should never be reduced below $V_{YSE}$ in an attempt to hold altitude.

Once it has been determined that an engine restart is not possible, the pilot should select the closest suitable airport in terms of time. Because of wind or other considerations, such as deteriorating weather, this may not be the closest airport in distance. Time is the prime factor if altitude cannot be maintained.

Although an extended period of flight is not recommended, it may be necessary to reach the destination or alternate airport. In this case, fuel from the wing tanks should be used evenly so the weight distribution on each side of the airplane remains equal. A fuel crossfeed is incorporated in the fuel system for this purpose and allows the pilot to select and use the fuel from the wing tanks on the side of the failed engine. The checklist should be studied carefully to determine the correct procedure for fuel crossfeed.

## LANDING

An engine-out landing in a multi-engine airplane requires a well planned approach so that the initial attempt is successful. Generally, the only differences between a twin-engine approach

and an engine-out approach are the size of the traffic pattern and the point at which the landing gear is extended.

A slightly larger traffic pattern may be flown to create shallower turns. The shallower turns provide better airplane control, better visibility and more time to plan for and monitor the approach.

Generally, the landing gear is not extended during the approach until the airplane is established at approach airspeed and the pilot is positively assured of reaching the desired runway. This timing is important since the extension of the landing gear adds sufficient drag to create a 300 to 500 f.p.m. rate of descent without a power reduction. However, it is important to allow sufficient time for a manual gear extension if the normal extension system fails. Some airplanes have hydraulic landing gear systems operated by only one hydraulic pump. If the hydraulic pump is installed on the inoperative engine, a manual extension is obviously required.

The wing flaps should be used as little as possible, preferably not at all until the landing gear is extended and the landing is assured. The pilot's operating handbook should be consulted to determine the maximum amount of flaps to be used during an engine-out landing.

## ENGINE-OUT REJECTED LANDING

A go-around from a rejected (balked) landing with one engine inoperative is advisable only under the best conditions of weight, altitude, and temperature. In fact, if the density altitude at the airport and the aircraft's weight are very high, a single-engine go-around may be impossible. For these reasons, the single-engine approach should be planned carefully so a go-around is not required.

If it appears a go-around may be necessary, a decision should be made early in the approach to either land or reject the landing. To make this decision, the pilot should consider aircraft performance, terrain contour, and heights of obstacles in the vicinity of the airport. Then, the pilot should establish a "go, no-go" altitude based on the altitude loss that occurs during the flap and gear retraction and the normal sink encountered during the transition to a single-engine climb. If a decision for a go-around is made before reaching this altitude, the pilot should add full power, retract the flaps and landing gear, and climb at $V_{YSE}$. After this speed is established, the aircraft is retrimmed for single-engine flight if the pilot desires.

If, however, the aircraft has descended below the go, no-go altitude, the pilot is generally *committed to land*. Under certain conditions, the pilot may be better off to land on the side of the runway, a parallel taxiway, or even the grass next to the runway, rather than to attempt a go-around. For specific procedures, multi-engine pilots should always refer to the POH of the training aircraft.

# ENGINE INOPERATIVE LOSS OF DIRECTIONAL CONTROL DEMONSTRATION

The purpose of this demonstration is to show the control pressures necessary to maintain directional control with one engine inoperative. The multi-engine pilot also will learn the correct recovery procedure when control can no longer be maintained. This demonstration should be accomplished

*Fig. 3-17. Stall Indication or Loss of Directional Control*

within a safe distance of a suitable airport and the entry altitude should allow completion no lower than 3,000 feet AGL. Since actual $V_{MC}$ varies with existing conditions, the pilot should not try to duplicate the published $V_{MC}$ which was established during initial aircraft certification.

Unfortunately, as speed decreases, yaw toward the inoperative engine is not the only control problem. The airplane also tends to roll into the inoperative engine, and this tendency becomes greater as airspeed is further reduced. Trying to counteract the rolling movement with aileron control aggravates the yawing tendency (the down aileron creates more drag than the up aileron). As shown in figure 3-17, if the airplane stalls in this situation, a violent roll into the inoperative engine may result. In this event, recovery should be started immediately by simultaneously reducing power on the operative engine and by decreasing the angle of attack. To avoid a stall, the pilot must remain at or above $V_{MC}$ at all times during engine-out operations.

As mentioned earlier, there is a density altitude above which the stalling speed is higher than the engine inoperative minimum control speed. When this density altitude exists close to the ground because of high elevation and/or high temperatures, an effective $V_{MC}$ demonstration may be hazardous and should not be attempted. This determination should be made before the flight.

If conditions indicate a $V_{MC}$ demonstration is practical, emphasis should be placed on conserving altitude. To begin, propellers are set at high r.p.m., the landing gear is retracted, and the cowl and wing flaps are set in the takeoff position. Then, the aircraft is placed in a climb attitude with the airspeed representative of that following a normal takeoff. Excessive nose-high pitch attitudes should be avoided because the airplane may become uncontrollable when power on the critical engine is reduced. Next, with both engines developing near rated takeoff power, the throttle on the critical engine, usually the left, is gradually reduced to idle (windmilling, not shut down). After this, airspeed should slowly be decreased with elevator or stabilator control pressure and a bank toward the good engine should be used for best performance. At the same time, the pilot applies rudder pressure to maintain directional control until the rudder is fully deflected. At the first indication of loss of directional control, recovery should be started immediately by reducing power on the operating engine while decreasing the angle of attack. After control is regained and airspeed is established at $V_{YSE}$, power may be added on the operative engine to complete the demonstration.

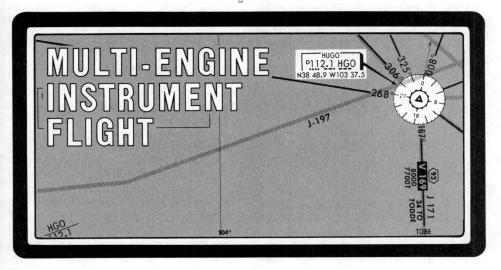

# chapter 4

# INTRODUCTION

Attitude instrument flying in a multi-engine airplane is basically the same as in a single-engine airplane. The main differences are related to the added systems complexity, greater operating parameters, and potential problems of engine-out operations. The ability to cope with these factors requires a high level of knowledge and skill, both during preflight planning and throughout the flight.

Multi-engine applicants who are instrument rated and want to exercise the privileges of the instrument rating in a multi-engine airplane, are required to demonstrate competency in instrument flight during the practical test. The required procedures include instrument flight with all engines operating and with one engine inoperative. Applicants should refer to the appropriate *Practical Test Standards* (private or commercial) for the specific maneuvers and performance criteria. Normal multi-engine instrument procedures are addressed in this section, and one engine inoperative multi-engine instrument procedures are discussed in Section B. For applicants who are not instrument rated or do not wish to demonstrate competency in instrument flight, multi-engine privileges are limited to VFR only.

# SECTION A — NORMAL PROCEDURES

Normal instrument procedures involve three fundamental skills — cross-check, instrument interpretation, and aircraft control. In a multi-engine airplane, the same skills are required, but higher operating speeds and the possibility of asymmetrical power make aircraft control more difficult.

## AIRCRAFT CONTROL

An essential element of aircraft control is learning the power settings required to maintain the desired airspeeds and attitudes in normal maneuvers and configurations. With two engines, overcontrolling on power changes is a common tendency during initial training. Most power adjustments are made using throttles (manifold pressure) rather than propeller controls. After a power change, the engines must be adjusted to produce equal power, which makes the task of maintaining a constant heading much easier.

When the power is properly set and the correct attitude is established, airplane performance is relatively predictable. However, since precise aircraft control is mandatory in the IFR environment, the pilot must learn to apply the required control pressures promptly and consistently. In addition to knowing the correct power settings, airspeeds, and attitudes, effective use of trim is required.

## USE OF TRIM

Trim is always important in instrument flying, and even more so in a high performance, multi-engine aircraft. Poor trim technique causes control pressures to become excessive and may lead to fatigue. Although trim technique varies with different airplanes, a common method involves using coarse trim to relieve the initial control pressure changes. Once the airplane is stabilized at the new attitude and/or airspeed, fine adjustments may then be made. A properly trimmed aircraft decreases the pilot's workload, allowing more time for the multiple tasks of instrument flight.

## USE OF EQUIPMENT

While certain limitations apply to all aircraft, multi-engine airplanes generally perform adequately and are well equipped for flight under IFR. Advanced avionics with multiple nav-comm radios, area navigation equipment, as well as flight director and autopilot systems, are common. Some airplanes have weather avoidance radar, cabin pressurization, and anti-icing or de-icing systems which increase their versatility.

A major challenge for pilots is to learn how to operate and use more sophisticated equipment effectively. If a pilot is unfamiliar with advanced instrumentation or equipment, these systems can become a distraction rather than an aid for decreasing the cockpit workload. On the practical test, a multi-engine applicant is required to exhibit knowledge of various systems and equipment malfunctions by explaining causes, indications, and pilot actions.

# IFR PLANNING

A typical IFR flight from one airport to another consists of several distinct phases — normally the departure, enroute, arrival, and approach phases. In a multi-engine aircraft, it is often possible to choose from a wide range of operating altitudes and airspeeds during most of the flight. Since different airspeeds, altitudes, and fuel consumption rates generally apply to different phases, flight planning must include separate computations for each phase. In many cases where weather is a factor, fuel economy is the main consideration; however, range or minimum time may be the primary planning concern for some flights.

## DEPARTURE

Prior to takeoff in marginal weather, the multi-engine pilot must carefully review the departure and associated procedures. For instance, what effect will a wet runway have on the airplane's accelerate-stop distance? Does the airport have a SID or a published departure procedure? What rate of climb is required? A takeoff should not be attempted when existing weather is below landing minimums, since an emergency could make it necessary to return to the departure airport for a landing. In addition, the pilot should be prepared to follow recommended procedures for engine failure on takeoff or during the climb. A systematic review of aircraft performance capabilities, including engine-out procedures, airspeeds, and climb limitations, should be accomplished before takeoff.

## ENROUTE

For the enroute phase, key planning decisions include selecting the route of flight and the cruising altitude(s), although aircraft performance and equipment limitations must also be considered. For example, the service ceiling, or lack of an appropriate oxygen system, could restrict a flight to lower altitudes. It is also a good practice to be aware of the facilities at airports along the route in case an emergency requires a landing short of the destination. The planning process should always include a thorough check of the enroute weather. Adverse conditions, such as icing, thunderstorms, turbulence, or even wind, often dictate a change in the route of flight and/or a particular altitude.

## ARRIVAL AND HOLDING

The transition from the enroute to the approach phase of an instrument flight involves changes in all flight parameters — altitude, heading, airspeed, and configuration. These changes are more significant in a multi-engine airplane due to the expanded operating envelope and more complex aircraft systems. The retractable landing gear and improved streamlining result in a slower deceleration when power is reduced, and the higher cruising altitude increases the time to make a comfortable, economical descent. Additional tasks, such as computing the rate of descent, requesting clearance, following ATC instructions, and reviewing the approach/missed approach procedures, increase the pilot's workload.

A pilot must also be prepared to enter the correct holding pattern and establish an appropriate holding airspeed. Although the maximum holding airspeed for propeller-driven aircraft is 175 KIAS, a slower airspeed may be recommended for several reasons — less fuel is required, altitude control is easier, and the holding pattern size decreases. Airspeed permitting, the first increment of flaps may be used to slow the airplane. The pilot's operating handbook usually includes information on holding airspeeds.

## INSTRUMENT APPROACH WITH ALL ENGINES OPERATING

Preplanning is an essential part of any instrument approach. This is especially true while training in a multi-engine airplane under the concept of single-pilot operations. A detailed study of the approach procedures for both the destination and alternate airports is an integral part of preflight preparation. Ideally, this means that when the pilot refers to an approach chart during flight, it is being reviewed rather than studied for the first time.

A single-pilot instrument approach requires several tasks to be performed in a relatively short time. This time span is compressed in a multi-engine airplane because of higher approach speeds. More detailed checklist procedures also increase the workload. As a result, the pilot must be well prepared, plan ahead, and organize the required tasks in a logical way. This systematic organization is one of the elements of cockpit management.

According to multi-engine practical test standards, the pilot is required to exhibit appropriate knowledge of cockpit management used for the published instrument approach. Additional criteria include the requirements to obtain a clearance, follow ATC instructions, and determine the appropriate rate of descent (considering wind and the missed approach point). The descent also must be accomplished on course to arrive at the DH or MDA in a position to complete a normal landing, either straight-in or circling. For an instrument approach with all engines operating, the pilot is also expected to properly execute a missed approach at the designated MAP and follow the airplane's cleanup checklist.

# SECTION B — INSTRUMENT PROCEDURES WITH ONE ENGINE INOPERATIVE

An engine failure is always critical, and it can be even more so during flight under instrument conditions. The multi-engine pilot must devote attention to emergency procedures and, at the same time, maintain control of the airplane by referring to the instruments. Because of this, it is imperative to understand and be able to recall engine-out procedures immediately.

## ENGINE FAILURE DURING STRAIGHT-AND-LEVEL FLIGHT AND TURNS

As indicated in the practical test standards, the pilot must recognize engine failure promptly, set the engine controls, reduce drag, and identify/verify the inoperative engine. Since the aircraft tends to yaw and roll toward the inoperative engine when an engine fails, the attitude indicator and turn coordinator will indicate a turn in the direction of the malfunctioning engine.

To maintain control, the pilot must establish the best engine-out airspeed and trim the airplane as required. The appropriate checklist procedures for securing the inoperative engine also must be accomplished. For the best performance in straight-and-level flight, a bank toward the operating engine is recommended. During a turn, bank angle must be monitored closely. Best turning performance is obtained in approximately a standard-rate turn.

When the airplane is fully under control and checklist procedures are completed, the pilot should attempt to determine the cause of the engine malfunction. Altitude should be conserved or a minimum sink rate should be established, depending on factors such as density altitude, service ceiling, aircraft weight, and elevation of terrain or obstructions. The pilot should also continue to monitor the operating engine and make adjustments as necessary.

In a training situation or during a practical test, engine failure is simulated as specified in the pilot's operating handbook. However, the simulated procedures closely parallel those of an actual engine failure. Applicants are required to maintain altitude, airspeed, and heading within the limits specified in the appropriate practical test standards (private or commercial). In addition, the multi-engine applicant is expected to be aware of engine-out performance capabilities and operating limitations, maintain positive control of the airplane at all times, and decide on a course of action to ensure a safe landing.

## INSTRUMENT APPROACH WITH ONE ENGINE INOPERATIVE

While an engine failure in a multi-engine airplane is a critical in-flight situation, the pilot may have some options — continue to the destination, land at the nearest airport, or land at the nearest suitable airport. The decision on the best course of action usually depends on factors such as the type of aircraft, probable cause of the engine failure, and altitude. As a general rule, it is advisable to land as soon as practical at a suitable airport. In an IFR environment, weather is a major consideration.

In most circumstances, the pilot should make sure a landing can be made on the first approach. A missed approach with one engine inoperative is difficult under the best conditions and, in many cases, it may be impossible. The decreased performance capability and asymmetrical thrust combine to make the engine-out missed approach a very undesirable maneuver, especially under instrument conditions.

If possible, the pilot should choose an airport with current and forecast weather well above the approach minimums. A precision approach should be used, when available. This type of approach provides accurate glide path information to touchdown and minimizes the need to maintain altitude for an extended time during the approach. Prolonged high power settings at low altitude should be avoided, if possible. If radar service is available, it should be requested. Radar vectors decrease the pilot's workload and usually reduce the

maneuvering and time required to fly the approach.

During the approach, the pilot must comply with the prescribed engine-out checklist procedures, including management of power, drag, airspeed, and trim. For a successful approach, the pilot also must use the published instrument approach procedure, follow ATC instructions, and maintain positive control of the airplane at all times.

When circumstances permit, the pilot should attempt to fly the approach like a normal all-engines-operating procedure. Deviations from a familiar routine can increase existing problems. As shown in figure 4-1, the airplane should be slowed to the recommended

Fig. 4-1. Instrument Approach — One Engine Inoperative

approach speed, but no lower than $V_{YSE}$, prior to intercepting the glide slope. The only recommended deviation from normal approach procedures pertains to the use of gear and flaps. As a general rule, the airplane should be established on course at the final approach fix with the gear and flaps in the UP position. Normally, they should not be fully extended until a safe landing is assured.

During the final approach, speed at or above $V_{YSE}$ is maintained. The final segment should be planned so a gradual power reduction on the operating engine will permit the touchdown to occur with the engine power at or near idle. This gradual change in power allows a smoother transition in rudder pressure changes and trim adjustments needed for directional control.

Performance criteria for an instrument approach with one engine inoperative are listed in practical test standards. Pilots are expected to descend on course and arrive at the DH or MDA, whichever is applicable, in a position from which a normal landing can be made. Compliance with normal instrument approach procedures is required.

As indicated earlier, most of the multi-engine procedures discussed in this text are general. Since certain procedures vary for different aircraft, pilots should always follow the recommendations in the POH for the airplane they are flying.

# EXERCISES

## INTRODUCTION

The exercises are designed to complement the *Multi-Engine Pilot Manual* and videocassette. Each exercise is correlated with a specific textbook chapter and section. For example, Exercise 1A applies to textbook Chapter 1, Section A.

The exercises include multiple choice, true/false, matching, and completion questions. To answer the multiple choice questions, circle the number of the correct choice. Fill in the appropriate blanks to answer the other questions. Further instructions may appear at the beginning of a section or within the body of an individual exercise, when necessary. The answers to all of the exercises are grouped at the back of the manual following the Pilot Briefing section.

## CHAPTER 1—MULTI-ENGINE OPERATIONS AND SYSTEMS

## Exercise 1A—Procedures And Maneuvers

1. _____ (True, False) Asymmetrical loading of the propellers contributes to the left-turning tendency in conventional multi-engine airplanes.

2. _____ (True, False) Torque contributes to a rolling moment in the same direction as propeller rotation.

3. If a rapid power reduction is made on a slow final approach, a high sink rate might be experienced because

   1. P-factor is reduced.
   2. the cowl flaps are open.
   3. induced airflow is reduced.
   4. torque is eliminated.

4. The V-speed which produces the best rate of climb in a twin-engine airplane is termed

   1. $V_X$.
   2. $V_Y$.
   3. $V_{XSE}$.
   4. $V_{YSE}$.

5. _____ (True, False) During taxi in a strong crosswind, power can be increased on the downwind engine to counteract the weathervaning tendency.

6. The altitude where $V_X$ and $V_Y$ converge is known as the _____ _____.

7. _____ (True, False) Turbocharging increases the service ceiling of an airplane by providing the engines with enough power to produce additional lift at higher altitudes.

**Complete the exercise below by matching the terms on the right, with the corresponding V-speed designations on the left.**

8. _____ $V_A$

9. _____ $V_{FE}$

10. _____ $V_{MC}$

11. _____ $V_{NE}$

12. _____ $V_{XSE}$

13. _____ $V_{YSE}$

14. _____ $V_{LE}$

15. _____ $V_{S1}$

16. _____ $V_{SO}$

17. _____ $V_{NO}$

18. _____ $V_Y$

19. _____ $V_X$

A.  Maximum flap extended speed
B.  Minimum control speed
C.  Best single-engine angle-of-climb speed
D.  Maneuvering speed
E.  Never-exceed speed
F.  Best multi-engine angle-of-climb speed
G.  Maximum structural cruising speed
H.  Best multi-engine rate-of-climb speed
I.  Maximum landing gear extended speed
J.  Stalling speed in landing configuration
K.  Best single-engine rate-of-climb speed
L.  Stalling speed in a specified configuration

**Arrange the items on the right in the proper preflight planning sequence.**

20. _____

21. _____

22. _____

23. _____

24. _____

A.  Consideration of terrain and obstructions
B.  Determination of the airplane's runway requirements
C.  Selection of alternatives in the event of engine failure
D.  Review of engine-out airspeeds
E.  Determination of density altitude

25. _____ (True, False) After a pilot has become familiar with a multi-engine airplane and has gained several hours of multi-engine flight experience, it is not necessary to refer to every item on the printed checklist.

26. _____ (True, False) When instruments or equipment are inoperative, the pilot has the option of using either the MEL or the provisions of FAR 91.213 in determining if the aircraft is airworthy.

27. The recommended procedure for making tight turns during taxi operations is to use

   1. nosewheel steering.
   2. differential braking.
   3. differential power.
   4. nosewheel steering and differential braking.

28. _____ (True, False) The recommended rotation speed for a normal takeoff in a twin-engine airplane is $V_{MC} \pm$ five knots.

29. If takeoff is initiated when the existing density altitude is higher than the single-engine service ceiling, an engine failure will result in a _____ _____ .

30. _____ (True, False) The possibility of an engine failure should be considered for every takeoff in a multi-engine airplane.

31. The safest procedure to follow when the accelerate-stop distance is longer than the available takeoff runway and the existing airport density altitude is higher than the single-engine service ceiling is to wait for more favorable winds and density altitude conditions and/or reduce gross weight by offloading _____ , _____ , or _____ .

32. During the takeoff run, the pilot should check the r.p.m., MAP, and oil pressure/temperature in addition to checking the

   1. fuel-flow indicators and the airspeed indicator.
   2. exhaust gas temperature gauges and fuel selectors.
   3. flight instruments and the fuel quantity gauges.
   4. the flap position indicator and the cabin door.

33. After liftoff during a normal takeoff, the most desirable climb speed is

   1. between $V_{XSE}$ and $V_{YSE}$.
   2. between $V_{MC}$ and cruise climb speed.
   3. $V_{YSE}$.
   4. $V_Y$.

34. During a normal takeoff, the point of gear retraction should occur

    1.  as soon as possible after liftoff.
    2.  when a positive rate of climb has been established and insufficient runway remains for landing.
    3.  as the airplane reaches a safe maneuvering altitude.
    4.  just prior to the first power reduction.

35. List methods which are beneficial in reducing excessively hot cylinder head temperatures during climbout.

    1.  _____
    2.  _____
    3.  _____
    4.  _____
    5.  _____

36. The most efficient and accurate method of adjusting the mixture at cruising altitude is through use of the

    1.  EGT gauge.
    2.  fuel-flow indicators.
    3.  propeller synchronization system.
    4.  power setting tables in the pilot's operating handbook.

37. Determine the number of nautical miles required to descend to the traffic pattern altitude under the following conditions.

    Cruising altitude . . . . . . . . . . . . . . . . . . . . . . . . . . . 15,500 ft. MSL
    Traffic pattern altitude . . . . . . . . . . . . . . . . . . . . . . . 1,500 ft. MSL
    Descent rate . . . . . . . . . . . . . . . . . . . . . . . . . . . . . . 700 f.p.m.
    Descent groundspeed . . . . . . . . . . . . . . . . . . . . . . . . . . 170 kts.

    1.  20 n.m.
    2.  37 n.m.
    3.  57 n.m.
    4.  63 n.m.

38. When should the prelanding checklist be completed?

    1.  Prior to entering the traffic pattern
    2.  Before turning base leg
    3.  During base leg
    4.  Anytime before short final approach

39. When should the propeller and mixture controls be placed in the full forward position during an approach?

    1.  At traffic pattern entry
    2.  During the prelanding check
    3.  While turning from base leg to final
    4.  Only when a go-around is imminent

40. _____ (True, False) A constant angle of descent is desirable during a maximum performance approach and landing.

41. _____ (True, False) It is seldom necessary to trim a multi-engine airplane during the performance of steep turns.

42. _____ (True, False) During practice of stall recognition, the first step in the recovery is an immediate, rapid power application at the first indication of aerodynamic buffeting.

43. List the three basic indications of an approach to a stall.

    1. _____
    2. _____
    3. _____

# Exercise 1B –
# General Systems

1. _____ (True, False) Propeller efficiency is determined mainly by the blade's angle of attack.

2. Aerodynamic forces acting on the blades of a spinning, constant speed propeller tend to twist the blades and _____ (increase, decrease) the angle of attack.

3. _____ (True, False) The propeller blade angle adjusts automatically to maintain a constant r.p.m. whenever a change in engine speed is sensed by the propeller governor.

4. The purpose of counterweights on a featherable propeller is to

    1. freeze the blade angle at the current setting in case of oil pressure loss.
    2. aid the propeller blades in moving towards high pitch.
    3. keep the propeller blades balanced during pitch changes.
    4. overcome the force of the compressed air in the feathering mechanism.

5. The two types of fuel pumps that provide fuel pressure to the engine are the _____-_____ and _____ _____ pumps.

6. _____ (True, False) Both types of fuel pumps should be checked prior to flight to ensure that they are operating properly.

7. _____ (True, False) All fuel passes through the fuel selector valve enroute from the tank to the engine.

8. Generally, the crossfeed system is utilized during extended _____
_____-_____ operations.

9. _____ (True, False) Fuel strainers and tanks are the only locations in fuel systems where quick drain valves are located.

10. _____ (True, False) The engine-driven fuel pump of a fuel injection system should be run only during landings, takeoffs, or when switching fuel tanks.

11. _____ (True, False) A fuel-flow indicator can be used in leaning the fuel-air ratio.

12. _____ (True, False) As compared to carburetor systems, fuel injection systems are less susceptible to induction icing and allow the greatest amount of vaporization cooling at the cylinder head.

13. _____ (True, False) Either a manually controlled or automatic alternate air source normally is provided on an airplane with a fuel injection system.

14. _____ (True, False) The AC electrical power that the alternators produce is converted to DC power within the reverse current relay switch.

**Match the basic electrical functions on the right with the associated system components on the left.**

15. _____ Voltage regulator

16. _____ Bus bar

17. _____ Overvoltage light

18. _____ Overvoltage relay

19. _____ Circuit breaker

A. Indicates the respective alternator is off the line

B. Protects the electrical system if the output exceeds maximum voltage

C. Distributes power throughout the electrical system

D. Maintains proper load sharing between alternators

E. Protects each component within the electrical system

20. A common power source for a retractable landing gear system is a
1. hydraulic hand pump.
2. vacuum-driven air pump.
3. one-way electric motor which drives a gearbox.
4. reversible electric motor which drives a hydraulic pump.

21. _____ (True, False) A blue radial line on the airspeed indicator marks the maximum speed for gear extension.

22. _____ (True, False) A common safety feature of landing gear indicator lights is the illumination of a red light when the gear is cycling or unsafe.

23. If the gear is not down and locked when the throttle is reduced below an established power setting, the pilots of some light twins are warned by a

_____ _____ _____.

24. _____ (True, False) Airspeed and pitch attitude are two flight characteristics which may provide an indication of a landing gear malfunction.

25. _____ (True, False) The turbocharger compressor is driven by exhaust gases and delivers pressurized air to the engine for high altitude operations.

26. _____ (True, False) Maximum rated manifold pressure is available when operating above the turbocharger's critical altitude.

27. _____ (True, False) To prevent overboosting some turbocharged engines, a pressure relief valve opens when the manifold pressure produced by the compressor is too high.

28. Wing de-icing and anti-icing equipment on most light, twin-engine airplanes may be classified as either _____ or _____ .

29. _____ (True, False) Anti-icing equipment should be turned on prior to entering icing conditions or at the first indication of icing.

30. The two methods of heat origination used in cabin heating systems are

_____ _____ _____ and _____

_____ _____.

# CHAPTER 2—PERFORMANCE CONSIDERATIONS

# Exercise 2A— Weight And Balance

**Match the weight and balance terms on the left with the correct descriptions on the right.**

1. _____ Maximum ramp weight

2. _____ Basic empty weight

3. _____ Maximum landing weight

4. _____ Center of gravity

5. _____ Reference datum

6. _____ Moment

7. _____ Maximum takeoff weight

8. _____ Arm

A. Weight of an item multiplied by its arm

B. Distance between the datum reference and a specific item in the airplane

C. The point at which an airplane would balance if suspended

D. The maximum weight approved for ground maneuvering (It includes the weight of start, taxi, and warm-up fuel.)

E. An arbitrarily fixed position along the longitudinal axis of the airplane from which distances are measured for purposes of weight and balance computations

F. Maximum weight at which takeoff is permitted

G. Weight of a standard airplane including unusable fuel, full operating fluids, full oil, and optional equipment

H. Maximum weight allowed for landing

9. The moment of an item that weighs 240 pounds and is positioned 133 inches aft of the datum reference is _____ lb.-in.

10. The total weight of a loaded airplane is 3,200 pounds and the total moment is 320,000 lb.-in.; therefore, the CG is located _____ inches aft of the datum.

11. _____ (True, False) Since the effects of overstressing an airplane are cumulative, structural failure may be caused by occasionally exceeding the maximum weight and load factor limitations.

12. The weight of 22.5 gallons of aviation fuel is approximately _____ pounds.

13. If the CG exceeds the aft limit, as the airspeed is reduced during the landing approach, the elevator or stabilator loses effectiveness and the nose may pitch _____ (up, down) uncontrollably.

14. The location of the airplane's center of gravity is found by dividing the total moment by the total _____.

15. The moment for the weight placed in a particular aircraft compartment is calculated by multiplying the weight in pounds times its distance in inches from the airplane's
    1. mean aerodynamic chord.
    2. engine compartment.
    3. main landing gear.
    4. datum reference.

16. _____ (True, False) To determine CG location when using a 1,000-pound index, the total moment must be multiplied times 1,000 before it is divided by total weight.

17. _____ (True, False) The advantage of reduction factors in weight and balance computations is a decrease in the size of the numbers.

18. An airplane with a CG location forward of limits will require a takeoff run which is _____ (longer, shorter) than normal.

19. What is the most dangerous condition for airplane weight and balance in terms of total weight and CG location?
    1. Over weight and CG forward of limits
    2. Over weight and CG aft of limits
    3. Under weight and CG forward of limits
    4. Under weight and CG aft of limits

**Use the weight and moment tables, and the weight and balance form for a typical six-place airplane to answer questions 20 through 23.**

## SAMPLE WEIGHT AND BALANCE FORM

| PAYLOAD COMPUTATIONS | | | | R E F | ITEM | | WEIGHT | MOMENT/ 100 |
|---|---|---|---|---|---|---|---|---|
| ITEM OCCUPANTS OR CARGO | ARM | WEIGHT | MOMENT/ 100 | 1. | BASIC EMPTY WEIGHT | | 3,472 | 1220.0 |
| | | | | 2. | PAYLOAD | | | |
| Seat 1 Seat 2 Seat 3 Seat 4 Seat 5 Seat 6 | | | | 3. | ZERO FUEL WEIGHT (sub-total) (Do not exceed maximum zero fuel weight) | | | |
| | | | | 4. | FUEL LOADING | (main) (auxiliary) (wing lockers) | | |
| BAGGAGE | | | | 5. | TAKEOFF WEIGHT | | | |
| PAYLOAD | | | | | | | | |
| | | | | 6. | LESS FUEL TO DESTINATION | (main) (auxiliary) (wing lockers) | | |
| | | | | 7. | LANDING WEIGHT | | | |

# WEIGHT AND MOMENT TABLES

## BAGGAGE

| WEIGHT (POUNDS) | NOSE COMPARTMENT ARM = -31" | WING LOCKER ARM = 63" | CABIN COMPARTMENTS | | |
|---|---|---|---|---|---|
| | | | ARM = 96" | ARM = 124" | ARM = 126" |
| | | MOMENT/100 | | | |
| 10 | -3 | 6 | 10 | 12 | 13 |
| 20 | -6 | 13 | 19 | 25 | 25 |
| 30 | -9 | 19 | 29 | 37 | 38 |
| 40 | -12 | 25 | 38 | 50 | 50 |
| 50 | -16 | 32 | 48 | 62 | 63 |
| 60 | -19 | 38 | 58 | 74 | 76 |
| 70 | -22 | 44 | 67 | 87 | 88 |
| 80 | -25 | 50 | 77 | 99 | 101 |
| 90 | -28 | 57 | 86 | 112 | 113 |
| 100 | -31 | 63 | 96 | 124 | 126 |
| 110 | -34 | 69 | 106 | 136 | 139 |
| 120 | -37 | 76 | 115 | 149 | 151 |
| 130 | -40 | 82 | 125 | 161 | 164 |
| 140 | -43 | 88 | 134 | 174 | 176 |
| 150 | -46 | 94 | 144 | 186 | 189 |
| 160 | -50 | 101 | 154 | 198 | 202 |
| 170 | -53 | 107 | 163 | | |
| 180 | -56 | 113 | 173 | | |
| 190 | -59 | 120 | 182 | | |
| 200 | -62 | 126 | 192 | | |
| 210 | -65 | 132 | 139 | | |
| 220 | -68 | 139 | | | |
| 230 | -71 | 145 | | | |
| 240 | -74 | 151 | | | |
| 250 | -78 | | | | |
| 260 | -81 | | | | |
| 270 | -84 | | | | |
| 280 | -87 | | | | |
| 290 | -90 | | | | |
| 300 | -93 | | | | |
| 310 | -96 | | | | |
| 320 | -99 | | | | |
| 330 | -102 | | | | |
| 340 | -105 | | | | |
| 350 | -108 | | | | |

## CREW AND PASSENGERS

| WEIGHT (POUNDS) | 1ST OR 2ND SEATS ARM = 37" | 3RD OR 4TH SEATS | | 5TH OR 6TH SEAT ARM = 102" |
|---|---|---|---|---|
| | | BENCH SEAT ARM = 71" | INDIVIDUAL SEAT ARM = 68" | |
| | | MOMENT/100 | | |
| 10 | 4 | 7 | 7 | 10 |
| 20 | 7 | 14 | 14 | 20 |
| 30 | 11 | 21 | 20 | 31 |
| 40 | 15 | 28 | 27 | 41 |
| 50 | 18 | 36 | 34 | 51 |
| 60 | 22 | 43 | 41 | 61 |
| 70 | 26 | 50 | 48 | 71 |
| 80 | 30 | 57 | 54 | 82 |
| 90 | 33 | 64 | 61 | 92 |
| 100 | 37 | 71 | 68 | 102 |
| 110 | 41 | 78 | 75 | 112 |
| 120 | 44 | 85 | 82 | 122 |
| 130 | 48 | 92 | 88 | 133 |
| 140 | 52 | 99 | 95 | 143 |
| 150 | 56 | 106 | 102 | 153 |
| 160 | 59 | 114 | 109 | 163 |
| 170 | 63 | 121 | 116 | 173 |
| 180 | 67 | 128 | 122 | 184 |
| 190 | 70 | 135 | 129 | 194 |
| 200 | 74 | 142 | 136 | 204 |
| 210 | 78 | 149 | 143 | 214 |
| 220 | 81 | 156 | 150 | 224 |
| 230 | 85 | 163 | 156 | 235 |
| 240 | 89 | 170 | 163 | 245 |
| 250 | 92 | 178 | 170 | 255 |
| 260 | 96 | 185 | 177 | 265 |
| 270 | 100 | 192 | 184 | 275 |
| 280 | 104 | 199 | 190 | 286 |
| 290 | 107 | 206 | 197 | 296 |
| 300 | 111 | 213 | 204 | 306 |

## FUEL

| GALLONS | WEIGHT (POUNDS) | MAIN WING TANKS ARM = 35" | AUXILIARY WING TANKS ARM = 47" | WING LOCKER TANKS ARM = 49" |
|---|---|---|---|---|
| | | MOMENT/100 | | |
| | | 10 | 14 | 15 |
| 5 | 30 | 10 | 14 | 15 |
| 10 | 60 | 21 | 28 | 29 |
| 15 | 90 | 32 | 42 | 44 |
| 20 | 120 | 42 | 56 | 59 |
| 25 | 150 | 52 | 70 | 74 |
| 30 | 180 | 63 | 85 | 88 |
| 35 | 210 | 74 | 99 | 103 |
| 40 | 240 | 84 | 113 | 118 |
| 45 | 270 | 94 | 127 | |
| 50 | 300 | 105 | 141 | |
| 55 | 330 | 116 | 155 | |
| 60 | 360 | 126 | 169 | |
| 63 | 378 | 132 | 178 | |
| 65 | 390 | 136 | | |
| 70 | 420 | 147 | | |
| 75 | 450 | 158 | | |
| 80 | 480 | 168 | | |
| 85 | 510 | 178 | | |
| 90 | 540 | 189 | | |
| 95 | 570 | 200 | | |
| 100 | 600 | 210 | | |

20. Compute the takeoff weight and CG location under the following conditions.

Maximum takeoff weight . . . . . . . . . . . . . . . . . 5,500 lbs.

Forward CG limit . . . . . . . . . . . . . . . . . . . 32.0 in.

Aft CG limit . . . . . . . . . . . . . . . . . . . . . 43.6 in.

Fuel loading

    Main . . . . . . . . . . . . . . . . . . . . . . 100 gals.

    Auxiliary . . . . . . . . . . . . . . . . . . . . 63 gals.

Baggage (Station 126) . . . . . . . . . . . . . . . . . 160 lbs.

Pilot (Seat 1) . . . . . . . . . . . . . . . . . . . . 180 lbs.

Passengers

    Seat 2 . . . . . . . . . . . . . . . . . . . . . 170 lbs.

    Seat 3 . . . . . . . . . . . . . . . . . . . . . 130 lbs.

    Seat 4 . . . . . . . . . . . . . . . . . . . . . 120 lbs.

    Seat 5 . . . . . . . . . . . . . . . . . . . . . 110 lbs.

    Seat 6 . . . . . . . . . . . . . . . . . . . . . 110 lbs.

The takeoff weight is _____ pounds and the CG is approximately _____ inches aft of the datum.

21. _____ (True, False) The airplane is within the CG limits for takeoff.

22. If the airplane burns a total of 85 gallons of fuel out of the main tanks and none out of the auxiliary tanks, what is the approximate CG for landing?

    1. 42.5 in.
    2. 43.0 in.
    3. 43.8 in.
    4. 44.1 in.

23. _____ (True, False) The airplane is within the CG limits for landing.

24. Assume an airplane is loaded out of CG limits and the pilot has determined some cargo must be moved from the aft compartment to the forward compartment. The following information is known.

Gross weight . . . . . . . . . . . . . . . . . . . . . . . . . . . . . . 4,500 lbs.
Forward CG limit . . . . . . . . . . . . . . . . . . . . . . . . . . . 33.0 in.
Aft CG limit . . . . . . . . . . . . . . . . . . . . . . . . . . . . . . 44.6 in.
Forward compartment . . . . . . . . . . . . . . . . . . . . . . . -10.0 in.
Aft compartment . . . . . . . . . . . . . . . . . . . . . . . . . . . 115.0 in.
Aft cargo . . . . . . . . . . . . . . . . . . . . . . . . . . . . . . . . 135 lbs.
Current CG . . . . . . . . . . . . . . . . . . . . . . . . . . . . . . . 45.5 in.

The minimum amount of weight that must be shifted to the forward compartment in order for the airplane to be within the CG limits is _____ pounds.

# Exercise 2B– Performance Charts

When necessary, see the charts at the end of this exercise for solutions to appropriate questions.

1. Use the altitude conversion chart to determine density altitude under the following conditions.

Pressure altitude . . . . . . . . . . . . . . . . . . . . . . . . . . . 3,000 ft.
Temperature . . . . . . . . . . . . . . . . . . . . . . . . . . . . . . 67°F

Density altitude is _____ feet.

2. Use the flight computer to determine the density altitude under the listed conditions.

Field elevation . . . . . . . . . . . . . . . . . . . . . . . . . . . . 6,100 ft.
Altimeter setting . . . . . . . . . . . . . . . . . . . . . . . . . . . 29.72
Temperature . . . . . . . . . . . . . . . . . . . . . . . . . . . . . . 86°F

The density altitude is

    1. 6,500 feet.
    2. 7,900 feet.
    3. 8,700 feet.
    4. 9,300 feet.

Match the operating conditions on the left with the corresponding effects on airplane performance on the right. Answers may be used more than once.

3. _____ Grass runway

4. _____ Uphill runway

5. _____ Hot day

6. _____ Light weight

7. _____ Low pressure altitude

A.  Increased takeoff distance
B.  Decreased landing distance
C.  Decreased maximum rate of climb

Match the atmospheric conditions on the left with the probable effects on density altitude on the right. Answers may be used more than once.

8. _____ Outside temperature of 15° Celsius at a field elevation of 3,000 feet MSL

9. _____ Altimeter setting of 30.12 at a field elevation of 4,000 feet MSL (assume standard temperature)

10. _____ Ground fog

11. _____ 10-knot headwind during takeoffs

A.  Density altitude above true altitude
B.  No effect on density altitude
C.  Density altitude below true altitude

To answer questions 12 through 14, use the appropriate charts with the following conditions. Consider each question independently.

Temperature . . . . . . . . . . . . . . . . . . . . . . . . . . . . . . 25°C
Pressure altitude . . . . . . . . . . . . . . . . . . . . . . . . . . 2,000 ft.
Headwind component . . . . . . . . . . . . . . . . . . . . . . 23 m.p.h.
Weight . . . . . . . . . . . . . . . . . . . . . . . . . . . . . . . . 4,300 lbs.

12.  The takeoff ground run for a short-field takeoff using 25° flaps is

1.  450 feet.
2.  550 feet.
3.  700 feet.
4.  900 feet.

13. The accelerate-stop distance with the flaps retracted is

    1.   2,100 feet.
    2.   2,410 feet.
    3.   2,470 feet.
    4.   2,530 feet.

14. The normal landing distance when landing over a 50-foot obstacle using 35° of flaps is

    1.   1,330 feet.
    2.   1,350 feet.
    3.   1,565 feet.
    4.   1,588 feet.

15. Determine the single-engine rate of climb from the appropriate chart using the listed conditions.

    Power setting . . . . . . . . . . . . . . . . . . . . . . . . . Maximum continuous
    Flaps . . . . . . . . . . . . . . . . . . . . . . . . . . . . . . . . . . . . Retracted
    Gear . . . . . . . . . . . . . . . . . . . . . . . . . . . . . . . . . . . . Extended
    Propeller . . . . . . . . . . . . . . . . . . . . . . . . . . . . . . . . Feathered
    Temperature . . . . . . . . . . . . . . . . . . . . . . . . . . . . 40° F
    Standard altitude . . . . . . . . . . . . . . . . . . . . . . . . 8,000 ft.
    Gross weight . . . . . . . . . . . . . . . . . . . . . . . . . . . 5,000 lbs.

    1.   335 f.p.m.
    2.   360 f.p.m.
    3.   535 f.p.m.
    4.   560 f.p.m.

16. Using the appropriate power setting tables, compute the manifold pressure, fuel flow, and true airspeed based on the following conditions.

    Power setting . . . . . . . . . . . . . . . . . . . . . . . . . . . . . 65%
    Temperature . . . . . . . . . . . . . . . . . . . . . . . . . . . . . +9°C
    Pressure altitude . . . . . . . . . . . . . . . . . . . . . . . . . . 13,000 ft.

    The manifold pressure is _____ in. Hg, the fuel flow is _____ g.p.h., and the true airspeed is _____ knots.

17. Determine the stalling speed in miles per hour for an airplane under the following conditions.

    Gross weight . . . . . . . . . . . . . . . . . . . . . . . . . . 3,900 lbs.
    Gear . . . . . . . . . . . . . . . . . . . . . . . . . . . . . . . . . Extended
    Flaps . . . . . . . . . . . . . . . . . . . . . . . . . . . . . . . . . Retracted

    1.   73 CAS
    2.   73 IAS
    3.   74 CAS
    4.   74 IAS

18. The values obtained from multi-engine airplane performance charts are based on

    1. a safety factor of 10 percent.
    2. average aircraft performance.
    3. maximum performance of a new aircraft.
    4. theoretical computations.

# ACCELERATE STOP DISTANCE

CONDITIONS:
1. Power - FULL THROTTLE and 2700 RPM Before Brake Release.
2. Mixtures - LEAN for field elevation
3. Wing Flaps - UP.
4. Cowl Flaps - OPEN.
5. Level, Hard Surface, Dry Runway.
6. Engine Failure at Engine Failure Speed.
7. Idle Power and Heavy Braking After Engine Failure.

NOTE:
1. If full power is applied without brakes set, distances apply from point where full power is applied.
2. Decrease distance 3% for each 4 knots headwind.
3. Increase distance 5% for each 2 knots tailwind.

| WEIGHT - POUNDS | ENGINE FAILURE SPEED - KIAS | PRESSURE ALTITUDE - FEET | TOTAL DISTANCE - FEET | | | | | | |
|---|---|---|---|---|---|---|---|---|---|
| | | | -20°C -4°F | -10°C +14°F | 0°C 32°F | +10°C +50°F | +20°C +68°F | +30°C +86°F | +40°C +104°F |
| 5500 | 92 | Sea Level | 3020 | 3190 | 3370 | 3550 | 3740 | 3930 | 4120 |
| | | 1000 | 3220 | 3400 | 3590 | 3790 | 3990 | 4210 | 4490 |
| | | 2000 | 3430 | 3630 | 3830 | 4050 | 4340 | 4570 | 4820 |
| | | 3000 | 3660 | 3880 | 4100 | 4400 | 4650 | 4910 | 5180 |
| | | 4000 | 3920 | 4160 | 4480 | 4730 | 5000 | 5290 | 5590 |
| | | 5000 | 4200 | 4530 | 4810 | 5090 | 5390 | 5700 | 6030 |
| | | 6000 | 4590 | 4880 | 5180 | 5490 | 5820 | 6170 | 6530 |
| | | 7000 | 4950 | 5270 | 5600 | 5940 | 6310 | 6700 | 7110 |
| | | 8000 | 5360 | 5710 | 6070 | 6460 | 6870 | 7310 | 7780 |
| | | 9000 | 5830 | 6210 | 6630 | 7060 | 7530 | 8020 | 8560 |
| | | 10,000 | 6330 | 6770 | 7230 | 7720 | 8250 | 8810 | 9420 |
| 5100 | 88 | Sea Level | 2540 | 2680 | 2830 | 2980 | 3140 | 3300 | 3470 |
| | | 1000 | 2710 | 2860 | 3020 | 3180 | 3350 | 3530 | 3710 |
| | | 2000 | 2880 | 3050 | 3220 | 3390 | 3580 | 3770 | 3970 |
| | | 3000 | 3070 | 3250 | 3440 | 3630 | 3830 | 4040 | 4330 |
| | | 4000 | 3290 | 3480 | 3680 | 3900 | 4190 | 4420 | 4660 |
| | | 5000 | 3520 | 3730 | 3950 | 4250 | 4500 | 4750 | 5020 |
| | | 6000 | 3770 | 4010 | 4320 | 4580 | 4850 | 5130 | 5430 |
| | | 7000 | 4060 | 4390 | 4660 | 4950 | 5240 | 5560 | 5890 |
| | | 8000 | 4470 | 4750 | 5050 | 5360 | 5690 | 6050 | 6420 |
| | | 9000 | 4840 | 5160 | 5490 | 5840 | 6220 | 6610 | 7030 |
| | | 10,000 | 5250 | 5600 | 5970 | 6370 | 6790 | 7230 | 7710 |
| 4700 | 85 | Sea Level | 2110 | 2230 | 2350 | 2470 | 2600 | 2740 | 2870 |
| | | 1000 | 2250 | 2370 | 2500 | 2640 | 2770 | 2920 | 3070 |
| | | 2000 | 2390 | 2520 | 2660 | 2810 | 2960 | 3120 | 3280 |
| | | 3000 | 2540 | 2690 | 2840 | 3000 | 3160 | 3340 | 3510 |
| | | 4000 | 2720 | 2880 | 3040 | 3210 | 3390 | 3580 | 3780 |
| | | 5000 | 2900 | 3080 | 3260 | 3440 | 3640 | 3840 | 4130 |
| | | 6000 | 3110 | 3300 | 3500 | 3700 | 3910 | 4210 | 4450 |
| | | 7000 | 3340 | 3550 | 3760 | 3990 | 4300 | 4550 | 4820 |
| | | 8000 | 3600 | 3830 | 4070 | 4390 | 4660 | 4940 | 5230 |
| | | 9000 | 3900 | 4230 | 4490 | 4770 | 5070 | 5380 | 5710 |
| | | 10,000 | 4300 | 4580 | 4870 | 5180 | 5510 | 5860 | 6240 |
| 4300 | 81 | Sea Level | 1730 | 1820 | 1920 | 2020 | 2120 | 2230 | 2340 |
| | | 1000 | 1830 | 1940 | 2040 | 2150 | 2260 | 2380 | 2500 |
| | | 2000 | 1950 | 2060 | 2170 | 2290 | 2410 | 2530 | 2660 |
| | | 3000 | 2070 | 2190 | 2310 | 2440 | 2570 | 2710 | 2850 |
| | | 4000 | 2210 | 2340 | 2470 | 2610 | 2750 | 2900 | 3060 |
| | | 5000 | 2360 | 2500 | 2640 | 2790 | 2950 | 3110 | 3280 |
| | | 6000 | 2520 | 2680 | 2830 | 2990 | 3160 | 3340 | 3530 |
| | | 7000 | 2710 | 2870 | 3040 | 3220 | 3410 | 3600 | 3880 |
| | | 8000 | 2910 | 3090 | 3280 | 3470 | 3680 | 3970 | 4200 |
| | | 9000 | 3140 | 3340 | 3550 | 3760 | 4070 | 4310 | 4570 |
| | | 10,000 | 3390 | 3610 | 3830 | 4150 | 4410 | 4680 | 4970 |

# NORMAL LANDING DISTANCE

CONDITIONS:
1. Throttles - IDLE.
2. Landing Gear - DOWN.
3. Wing Flaps - 35°.
4. Cowl Flaps - CLOSE.
5. Level, Hard Surface Runway.
6. Maximum Braking Effort.

NOTE:
1. Increase distance by 25% of ground run for operation on firm sod runway.
2. If necessary to land with wing flaps UP, the approach speed should be increased above the normal approach speed by 12 knots. Expect total landing distance to increase by 35%.
3. Decrease total distances by 3% for each 4 knots headwind. For operations with tailwinds up to 10 knots, increase total distances by 5% for each 2 knots wind.

| WEIGHT- POUNDS | SPEED AT 50-FOOT OBSTACLE KIAS | PRESSURE ALTITUDE - FEET | 20°C (68°F) | | 30°C (86°F) | | 40°C (104°F) | |
|---|---|---|---|---|---|---|---|---|
| | | | GROUND ROLL - FEET | TOTAL DISTANCE TO CLEAR 50-FOOT OBSTACLE | GROUND ROLL - FEET | TOTAL DISTANCE TO CLEAR 50-FOOT OBSTACLE | GROUND ROLL - FEET | TOTAL DISTANCE TO CLEAR 50-FOOT OBSTACLE |
| 5400 | 93 | Sea Level | 660 | 1810 | 680 | 1830 | 700 | 1850 |
| | | 1000 | 680 | 1830 | 700 | 1850 | 730 | 1880 |
| | | 2000 | 710 | 1860 | 730 | 1880 | 750 | 1900 |
| | | 3000 | 730 | 1880 | 760 | 1910 | 780 | 1930 |
| | | 4000 | 760 | 1910 | 780 | 1930 | 810 | 1960 |
| | | 5000 | 790 | 1940 | 810 | 1960 | 840 | 1990 |
| | | 6000 | 820 | 1970 | 850 | 2000 | 870 | 2020 |
| | | 7000 | 850 | 2000 | 880 | 2030 | 910 | 2060 |
| | | 8000 | 880 | 2030 | 910 | 2060 | 940 | 2090 |
| | | 9000 | 920 | 2070 | 950 | 2100 | 980 | 2130 |
| | | 10,000 | 950 | 2100 | 980 | 2130 | 1020 | 2170 |
| 5000 | 89 | Sea Level | 550 | 1700 | 570 | 1720 | 590 | 1740 |
| | | 1000 | 570 | 1720 | 590 | 1740 | 610 | 1760 |
| | | 2000 | 600 | 1750 | 620 | 1770 | 640 | 1790 |
| | | 3000 | 620 | 1770 | 640 | 1790 | 660 | 1810 |
| | | 4000 | 640 | 1790 | 660 | 1810 | 680 | 1830 |
| | | 5000 | 670 | 1820 | 690 | 1840 | 710 | 1860 |
| | | 6000 | 690 | 1840 | 710 | 1860 | 740 | 1890 |
| | | 7000 | 720 | 1870 | 740 | 1890 | 770 | 1920 |
| | | 8000 | 750 | 1900 | 770 | 1920 | 800 | 1950 |
| | | 9000 | 770 | 1920 | 800 | 1950 | 830 | 1980 |
| | | 10,000 | 800 | 1950 | 830 | 1980 | 860 | 2010 |
| 4600 | 86 | Sea Level | 460 | 1610 | 480 | 1630 | 490 | 1640 |
| | | 1000 | 480 | 1630 | 500 | 1650 | 510 | 1660 |
| | | 2000 | 500 | 1650 | 510 | 1660 | 530 | 1680 |
| | | 3000 | 520 | 1670 | 530 | 1680 | 550 | 1700 |
| | | 4000 | 530 | 1680 | 550 | 1700 | 570 | 1720 |
| | | 5000 | 550 | 1700 | 570 | 1720 | 590 | 1740 |
| | | 6000 | 580 | 1730 | 600 | 1750 | 610 | 1760 |
| | | 7000 | 600 | 1750 | 620 | 1770 | 640 | 1790 |
| | | 8000 | 620 | 1770 | 640 | 1790 | 660 | 1810 |
| | | 9000 | 650 | 1800 | 670 | 1820 | 690 | 1840 |
| | | 10,000 | 670 | 1820 | 690 | 1840 | 720 | 1870 |
| 4200 | 82 | Sea Level | 380 | 1530 | 390 | 1540 | 410 | 1560 |
| | | 1000 | 390 | 1540 | 410 | 1560 | 420 | 1570 |
| | | 2000 | 410 | 1560 | 420 | 1570 | 440 | 1590 |
| | | 3000 | 420 | 1570 | 440 | 1590 | 450 | 1600 |
| | | 4000 | 440 | 1590 | 450 | 1600 | 470 | 1620 |
| | | 5000 | 460 | 1610 | 470 | 1620 | 490 | 1640 |
| | | 6000 | 470 | 1620 | 490 | 1640 | 500 | 1650 |
| | | 7000 | 490 | 1640 | 510 | 1660 | 520 | 1670 |
| | | 8000 | 510 | 1660 | 530 | 1680 | 540 | 1690 |
| | | 9000 | 530 | 1680 | 550 | 1700 | 560 | 1710 |
| | | 10,000 | 550 | 1700 | 570 | 1720 | 590 | 1740 |

## SINGLE ENGINE CLIMB
### STANDARD DAY (ISA)

ASSOCIATED CONDITIONS:

| | |
|---|---|
| POWER | MAXIMUM CONTINUOUS |
| FLAPS | UP |
| GEAR | UP |
| CLIMB SPEED | IAS AS TABULATED |
| INOPERATIVE PROPELLER | FEATHERED |

NOTE: DECREASE RATE-OF-CLIMB 25 FT/MIN FOR EACH 10°F ABOVE STANDARD DAY (ISA) TEMPERATURE.

| WEIGHT POUNDS | CLIMB SPEED MPH ~ IAS |
|---|---|
| 5990 | 122 |
| 5500 | 119 |
| 5000 | 116 |
| 4500 | 113 |

| CONFIGURATION | APPROXIMATE RATE-OF-CLIMB LOSS ~ FT/MIN |
|---|---|
| GEAR DOWN PROP WINDMILLING | 200 |
| GEAR DOWN AND PROP WINDMILLING | 200 |
| | 400 |

## CRUISE POWER SETTINGS

### 65% MAXIMUM CONTINUOUS POWER (OR FULL THROTTLE)

| PRESS ALT. | ISA-36°F (-20°C) | | | | | | | STANDARD DAY (ISA) | | | | | | | ISA +36°F (+20°C) | | | | | | |
|---|---|---|---|---|---|---|---|---|---|---|---|---|---|---|---|---|---|---|---|---|---|
| | OAT | ENGINE SPEED | MAN. PRESS | FUEL FLOW PER ENGINE | | TAS | | OAT | ENGINE SPEED | MAN. PRESS | FUEL FLOW PER ENGINE | | TAS | | OAT | ENGINE SPEED | MAN PRESS | FUEL FLOW PER ENGINE | | TAS | |
| FEET | °C | RPM | IN HG | PPH | GPH | KTS | MPH | °C | RPM | IN HG | PPH | GPH | KTS | MPH | °C | RPM | IN HG | PPH | GPH | KTS | MPH |
| SL | -5 | 2500 | 28.9 | 112 | 18.6 | 173 | 199 | 15 | 2500 | 29.8 | 112 | 18.6 | 177 | 204 | 35 | 2500 | 30.6 | 112 | 18.6 | 180 | 207 |
| 2000 | -9 | 2500 | 28.9 | 112 | 18.6 | 176 | 203 | 11 | 2500 | 29.8 | 112 | 18.6 | 180 | 207 | 31 | 2500 | 20.7 | 112 | 18.6 | 183 | 211 |
| 4000 | -13 | 2500 | 29.0 | 112 | 18.6 | 179 | 206 | 7 | 2500 | 29.8 | 112 | 18.6 | 183 | 211 | 27 | 2500 | 30.9 | 112 | 18.6 | 186 | 214 |
| 6000 | -17 | 2500 | 29.0 | 112 | 18.6 | 182 | 209 | 3 | 2500 | 29.9 | 112 | 18.6 | 186 | 214 | 23 | 2500 | 31.0 | 112 | 18.6 | 190 | 219 |
| 8000 | -21 | 2500 | 29.2 | 112 | 18.6 | 185 | 213 | -1 | 2500 | 30.0 | 112 | 18.6 | 189 | 218 | 19 | 2500 | 31.1 | 112 | 18.6 | 193 | 222 |
| 10000 | -25 | 2500 | 29.2 | 112 | 18.6 | 188 | 216 | -5 | 2500 | 30.2 | 112 | 18.6 | 193 | 222 | 15 | 2500 | 31.2 | 112 | 18.6 | 197 | 227 |
| 12000 | -29 | 2500 | 29.2 | 112 | 18.6 | 192 | 221 | -9 | 2500 | 30.3 | 112 | 18.6 | 196 | 226 | 11 | 2500 | 31.4 | 112 | 18.6 | 200 | 230 |
| 14000 | -33 | 2500 | 29.2 | 112 | 18.6 | 195 | 224 | -13 | 2500 | 30.4 | 112 | 18.6 | 200 | 230 | 7 | 2500 | 31.5 | 112 | 18.6 | 204 | 235 |
| 16000 | -37 | 2500 | 29.3 | 112 | 18.6 | 199 | 229 | -17 | 2500 | 30.5 | 112 | 18.6 | 204 | 235 | 3 | 2500 | 31.6 | 112 | 18.6 | 208 | 239 |
| 18000 | -41 | 2500 | 29.3 | 112 | 18.6 | 202 | 233 | -21 | 2500 | 30.6 | 112 | 18.6 | 207 | 238 | -1 | 2500 | 31.7 | 112 | 18.6 | 212 | 244 |
| 20000 | -44 | 2500 | 29.4 | 112 | 18.6 | 206 | 237 | -24 | 2500 | 30.6 | 112 | 18.6 | 211 | 243 | -4 | 2500 | 31.8 | 112 | 18.6 | 216 | 249 |
| 22000 | -48 | 2500 | 29.5 | 112 | 18.6 | 211 | 243 | -28 | 2500 | 30.8 | 112 | 18.6 | 216 | 249 | -8 | 2500 | 32.0 | 112 | 18.6 | 221 | 254 |
| 24000 | -53 | 2500 | 29.8 | 112 | 18.6 | 215 | 247 | -33 | 2500 | 31.1 | 112 | 18.6 | 220 | 253 | -13 | 2500 | 32.0 | 111 | 18.5 | 224 | 258 |
| 26000 | -57 | 2500 | 30.0 | 112 | 18.6 | 219 | 252 | -37 | 2500 | 31.3 | 112 | 18.6 | 225 | 259 | -17 | 2500 | 32.0 | 109 | 18.2 | 227 | 261 |
| 28000 | -61 | 2500 | 29.9 | 110 | 18.3 | 222 | 256 | -41 | 2500 | 29.9 | 105 | 17.5 | 223 | 257 | -21 | 2500 | 29.9 | 100 | 16.7 | 223 | 257 |
| 30000 | -64 | 2500 | 26.4 | 94 | 15.7 | 210 | 242 | -44 | 2500 | 26.4 | 91 | 15.1 | 210 | 242 | -24 | 2500 | 26.4 | 88 | 14.7 | 206 | 237 |

# CHAPTER 3—ENGINE-OUT OPERATIONS

# Exercise 3A– Aerodynamics

1. _____ (True, False) According to FAR Part 23, a light twin-engine airplane weighing 5,500 pounds gross weight and having a $V_{SO}$ of 58 knots is required to demonstrate a climb rate of at least 50 f.p.m. at 5,000 feet.

2. _____ (True, False) The left engine is the critical engine in all twin-engine airplanes.

3. _____ (True, False) Minimum control speed decreases as altitude increases.

4. _____ (True, False) Right engine failure in a conventional twin-engine airplane creates more control difficulties than failure of the left engine.

5. _____ (True, False) Lack of induced airflow after engine failure will cause the airplane to roll in the direction of the inoperative engine.

6. If an engine-out climb is not possible, the slowest rate of descent can be attained by using the single-engine best _____-of-climb airspeed.

7. If an engine-out climb is not possible, it is because

    1.   lift exceeds drag.
    2.   drag exceeds thrust.
    3.   thrust is greater than lift.
    4.   drag and lift are equal.

8. What critical speed for a multi-engine aircraft decreases as altitude increases?

    1.   $V_X$
    2.   $V_{XSE}$
    3.   $V_{MC}$
    4.   $V_{SSE}$

9. The least amount of drag is created when the propeller of the inoperative engine is

    1.   windmilling.
    2.   feathered.
    3.   stopped with a low blade angle.
    4.   stopped with a high blade angle.

10. When an aircraft is at a high angle-of-attack, the descending blade of the propeller is asymmetrically loaded because

    1.  it produces more thrust than the ascending blade.
    2.  it is heavier than the ascending blade.
    3.  the propeller has three blades.
    4.  the ascending blade creates more effective torque.

**Match the choice on the right with the corresponding term on the left.**

11. _____ Single-engine service ceiling

12. _____ Single-engine absolute ceiling

13. _____ Induced drag

14. _____ Critical engine

15. _____ Minimum control speed

16. _____ Single-engine best rate-of-climb

17. _____ High parasite drag

A.  Caused by a windmilling propeller

B.  That engine whose failure most adversely affects performance

C.  Maximum density altitude at which $V_{YSE}$ produces a 50 f.p.m. rate of climb

D.  That airspeed below which directional control cannot be maintained with one engine out and the other developing takeoff power

E.  Maximum density altitude the airplane is capable of attaining or maintaining

F.  Airspeed that produces the least rate of descent with the operating engine at maximum continuous power

G.  Caused by control surface deflection

18. Select the true statement regarding which factor causes the greatest amount of drag during an engine-out situation.

    1.  Extension of the landing gear
    2.  Extension of full flaps
    3.  Windmilling propeller
    4.  Unique to the specific type of multi-engine airplane

# Exercise 3B– Procedures And Maneuvers

1. _____ (True, False) If an engine is producing only partial power, it should be considered a failed engine and shut down immediately.

2. Immediately following an engine failure, the pilot's primary concern is to
   1. identify the inoperative engine.
   2. feather the propeller.
   3. maintain aircraft control.
   4. apply maximum power.

3. The first indication of an engine failure is a pronounced yaw towards the _____ (operative, inoperative) engine.

4. _____ (True, False) To verify that the failed engine has been identified correctly, the pilot should place the appropriate mixture control in the idle cutoff position.

5. If an engine failure occurs during the takeoff ground run before the single-engine minimum control speed is reached, the pilot should
   1. accelerate the airplane to $V_{XSE}$ on the ground and continue the takeoff.
   2. place both mixtures in idle cutoff and apply full flaps for aerodynamic braking.
   3. feather both propellers and apply the brakes, if necessary.
   4. discontinue the takeoff by closing both throttles and apply heavy braking, if required.

6. If an engine-out climb is not possible, the slowest rate of descent can be attained by using the single-engine best _____-of-climb airspeed.

7. When one engine is inoperative, the primary aerodynamic control used to overcome yaw is the _____.

8. _____ (True, False) During an engine-out approach to a landing, a higher-than-normal approach speed is maintained.

9. _____ (True, False) If an engine failure occurs during climb, the use of $V_{XSE}$ will produce a greater rate of climb than that produced by $V_{YSE}$.

10. _____ (True, False) During an engine-out approach, the wing flaps should be used as little as possible, preferably not at all until the landing is assured.

11. The two most critical phases of flight in a multi-engine airplane are
_____ and _____.

12. _____ (True, False) During the climb immediately following liftoff, attaining airspeed in excess of the multi-engine best rate-of-climb speed is not as valuable as gaining altitude.

13. If an engine failure occurs at the multi-engine service ceiling, the pilot may expect the airplane to drift down to the single-engine _____ ceiling.

14. The most frequent cause of an enroute engine failure is

    1.   an internal mechanical failure.
    2.   an ignition failure.
    3.   a lubrication malfunction.
    4.   interrupted fuel flow.

15. If an engine fails while enroute, the alternate airport which is selected should be the closest in terms of _____.

16. During the takeoff, the most critical point for an engine failure to occur is

    1.   prior to reaching $V_{MC}$.
    2.   between $V_{MC}$ and $V_{YSE}$.
    3.   between $V_{YSE}$ and $V_Y$.
    4.   after reaching $V_{XSE}$ but before reaching obstacle clearance altitude.

17. Assume an engine-out landing approach is being performed with the right engine inoperative and the airplane trimmed for straight flight. When the left throttle is closed during the landing flare, pressure will be required on the _____ (right, left) rudder pedal.

18. _____ (True, False) During an engine-out approach to landing, a higher-than-normal approach angle is maintained on final approach.

19. List three methods of identifying an inoperative engine.

    1.  _____
    2.  _____
    3.  _____

20. List, in sequence, the power settings which should be applied immediately following an engine failure.

    1.  _____
    2.  _____
    3.  _____

# CHAPTER 4—MULTI-ENGINE INSTRUMENT FLIGHT

## Exercise 4A—Normal Procedures

1. _____ (True, False) Attitude instrument flying in a multi-engine airplane is basically the same as in a single-engine airplane.

2. Failure to use appropriate trim procedures during airspeed and/or attitude changes may lead to _____ .

3. On a practical test, multi-engine applicants are required to exhibit knowledge of various systems and equipment malfunctions by explaining causes, indications, and _____ _____ .

4. Although not specifically prohibited for Part 91 operations, a takeoff under IFR should not be attempted when the weather at the departure airport is _____ _____ _____ .

5. Systematic organization of the required tasks during an instrument approach with all engines operating is referred to as _____ _____ .

6. With all engines operating during an instrument approach, an applicant on a practical test is expected to properly identify the MAP and execute a(n) _____ _____ .

## Exercise 4B—Instrument Procedures With One Engine Inoperative

**Questions 1 through 5 in this section pertain to an instrument approach with one engine inoperative.**

1. A go-around _____ (is, is not) recommended.

2. The only recommended deviation from normal instrument approach procedures concerns the use of _____ and _____ .

3. If the pilot has a choice, a _____ (precision, nonprecision) approach should be used.

4. When available, radar vectors _____ (should, should not) be requested.

5. On the final approach, airspeed should be no lower than _____ .

6. _____ (True, False) Since multi-engine procedures vary for different aircraft, the pilot should refer to the appropriate pilot's operating handbook.

# PILOT BRIEFINGS

## INTRODUCTION

Pilot briefings are a series of essay-type questions designed to provoke further study and discussion of training concepts. Each briefing relates to the corresponding subject area in the text. Prior to the briefing session, the applicant should complete the appropriate exercise by writing the answer to each question on a separate sheet of paper. During the briefing, the applicant and instructor should review each question and answer, then discuss related information. Answers to most of the pilot briefing questions are found in the textbook, while others may be found in the pilot's operating handbook or other appropriate publication. A series of multi-engine oral questions is included at the end of the pilot briefing section. These questions are designed to help the applicant prepare for the practical test.

## MULTI-ENGINE OPERATIONS AND SYSTEMS
### PROCEDURES AND MANEUVERS

1. Explain the elements contributing to the left-turning tendency in a conventional twin with both engines operating.

2. Explain the uses of differential power during taxi and takeoff.

3. Why are the effects of torque eliminated in airplanes with counter-rotating propellers?

4. How is asymmetrical loading of the propeller affected by angle of attack?

5. What factors limit the operating altitudes of light twin-engine airplanes?

6. Explain the difference between $V_X$ and $V_Y$.

7. How is power affected by altitude, for both normally aspirated and turbocharged engines?

8. Why does torque cause a rolling moment in conventional twin-engine airplanes?

9. Why does loss of induced airflow cause a loss of total lift?

10. Begin with the slowest V-speed that is shown on the airspeed indicator and describe each speed in order, including its significance.

11. Describe the preflight planning considerations necessary for a typical multi-engine cross-country flight.

12. Describe the important aspects of takeoff planning.

13. Should a takeoff be initiated when the accelerate-stop distance under existing conditions exceeds the length of the available runway?

14. Should a takeoff be initiated when the existing airport density altitude is higher than the single-engine service ceiling?

15. Describe the correct procedures and sequence of events for a normal takeoff.

16. Explain the correct procedures and sequence of events for performing a maximum performance takeoff.

17. Describe the proper course of action that must be taken when an engine failure occurs during take-off.

18. What guidelines normally determine the point of gear retraction following liftoff?

19. When is the first power reduction normally made during departure?

20. Which is more valuable during initial climb, airspeed in excess of $V_Y$ or altitude? Why?

21. What determines the configuration of the cowl flaps during a climb?

22. What are the advantages of performing a cruise climb to altitude?

23. Assuming full fuel tanks at departure, what is the sequence of fuel management throughout a cross-country flight?

24. Explain the factors involved in planning the descent to the destination airport.

25. Explain the correct procedures and sequence of events for a normal approach and landing.

26. Explain the correct procedures and sequence of events for a maximum performance landing over an obstacle.

27. During a maximum performance landing, what speed is used on the final approach? How does this speed compare with the single-engine minimum control speed?

28. Describe the correct procedures for performing a go-around from short final approach.

29. Explain the procedure for establishing flight at minimum controllable airspeed. What determines whether or not the aircraft is at minimum controllable airspeed?

30. Explain the procedures for setting up and executing imminent stalls in the approach-to-landing and take-off-and-departure configurations.

## GENERAL SYSTEMS

1. Explain how a constant speed propeller operates on a multi-engine airplane.

2. Explain how to use the propeller control lever.

3. What happens when the propeller control lever is moved to the full aft position?

4. What are the maximum continuous operating power settings for the training airplane? Why is it important to comply with these limitations?

5. Explain the procedures involved with power application or reduction.

6. Explain the propeller synchronizing system.

7. Is an autofeather system installed on the training airplane? If so, explain how the system works.

8. How does a reversible propeller system work? Can it be used in flight?

9. Diagram and explain the fuel system used in the training airplane.

10. Explain the type of pumps available to provide fuel pressure to the engines.

11. Explain the operation of the fuel selector control.

12. Explain the crossfeed system on the training airplane. When is it generally used?

13. For what purpose are fuel tank vents installed?

14. What is the purpose of fuel strainers, or gascolators?

15. Where are the quick drains located?

16. What is the normal fuel pressure and what are some of the things that will cause low pressure?

17. Explain the fuel injection system.

18. Explain the primary sources of electrical power.

19. What is the function of a voltage regulator?

20. Explain the purpose of an over-voltage relay.

21. How is electrical power distributed through the airplane?

22. Explain what adjustments have to be made with one alternator inoperative.

23. Explain the landing gear system used on the training airplane.

24. Explain the safety features designed into the landing gear system.

25. How is emergency landing gear extension accomplished?

26. Explain turbocharging and the operational characteristics of this type of system.

27. Explain the following ice control systems, if installed on the training airplane.
    1. Propeller
    2. Wing and tail surfaces
    3. Windshield

28. What type of cabin heating system is installed on the training airplane?

29. Explain how the cabin heating system operates.

30. How is the temperature in the cabin regulated?

# PERFORMANCE CONSIDERATIONS

## WEIGHT AND BALANCE

1. For the training airplane, what are the maximum ramp weight, maximum takeoff, maximum landing, and basic empty weights?

2. Which weights are required for weight computations?

3. Where is the basic empty weight found?

4. Which items are included in the payload?

5. What guidelines are used for making weight and balance computations if the weights of the passengers are unknown?

6. What is zero fuel weight?

7. Does the training airplane have a maximum zero fuel weight?

8. What is the purpose of a maximum zero fuel weight?

9. How does exceeding weight limits affect airplane performance?

10. Which item is used most often to adjust weight within limits when the plane has been overloaded?

11. Explain the following terms.
    1. Center of gravity
    2. Reference datum
    3. Arm
    4. Moment

12. What are three methods used to determine the center of gravity of an airplane?

13. Which method is used for the training airplane?

14. If the airplane is loaded to maximum capacity, will the greatest movement in center of gravity occur when weight is shifted from the fuel, baggage, or passenger loading station?

15. Assuming the listed conditions, determine whether the airplane is loaded within the center of gravity range.

    Pilot and front passenger. . .340 lbs.
    Rear passengers . . . . . 370 lbs.
    Fuel tanks . . . . . . . . . . Full
    Baggage . . . . . . . . . . .95 lbs.

16. Assuming that the airplane is loaded with the CG at the extreme aft limit, explain the handling characteristics of the airplane during normal operations, such as takeoffs and landings.

## PERFORMANCE CHARTS

1. Given the following conditions, determine the accelerate-stop distance, the normal takeoff ground run, and the takeoff distance necessary to clear a 50-foot obstacle.

   Field elevation . . . . .    2,000 ft.
   Temperature . . . . . . .      87°F
   Altimeter setting  . . . . .  29.72
   Runway . . . . . .  Hard surfaced
   Weight . . . . . .  Maximum gross
   Headwind component . . 10 m.p.h.

2. Assuming the airplane is loaded to maximum gross weight, compute the average rate of climb between the pressure altitudes of 5,000 and 10,000 feet if the temperature is 60° F at both altitudes.

3. Determine the calibrated and indicated stalling speeds under the following conditions.

    Angle of bank . . . . . . . . 50°
    Gear . . . . . . . . . . Extended
    Flaps . . . . . . . . . Retracted

4. Given the following conditions, determine the normal landing roll and the landing distance over a 50-foot obstacle.

    Field elevation . . . . . 3,500 ft.
    Temperature . . . . . . . . 82° F
    Altimeter setting . . . . . 30.32
    Weight . . . . . . Maximum gross

5. Determine the power settings that will provide 65 percent rated horsepower under the following conditions.

    Pressure altitude . . . . 7,000 ft.
    Temperature . . . . . . . . 64° F

6. What are the single-engine minimum control speed and single-engine absolute ceiling for the training airplane? What is the significance of each of these values?

# ENGINE-OUT OPERATIONS

## AERODYNAMICS

1. Define critical engine.

2. Does partial power loss affect $V_{MC}$? Why? Does altitude affect $V_{MC}$? Why?

3. Explain why airplanes with counterrotating propellers do not have a critical engine.

4. Why is the airplane directionally uncontrollable during flight below $V_{MC}$?

5. Why should the propeller of the inoperative engine be feathered if it cannot be restarted immediately?

6. How does asymmetrical loading of the propeller affect directional stability during single-engine operation?

7. Identify and explain all the factors that contribute to the rolling tendency of the airplane in the direction of the inoperative engine.

8. Explain why some airplanes may not be able to maintain altitude after engine failure.

9. Explain how loading and balance can affect $V_{MC}$.

10. Why does a 50 percent reduction of power cause an approximate 80 percent decrease in climb performance?

11. How is performance affected during an attempt to restart a failed engine with the propeller feathered?

12. Explain the operational significance of the single-engine service ceiling and the single-engine absolute ceiling.

13. How are $V_{YSE}$ and $V_{XSE}$ related to single-engine ceilings?

14. What guidelines should be followed when making turns with one engine inoperative?

15. Explain the relative order of drag factors during engine-out operations as they apply to the training airplane.

16. In terms of single-engine operation, what are the advantages of reducing operating gross weights?

17. Explain the effect of a turn on the production of induced drag.

18. What are the relative advantages of multi-engine airplanes equipped with counterrotating propellers compared to conventional twins in terms of engine-out operations and performance?

19. Explain the relationship between excess thrust available and total drag as they relate to engine-out climbs.

20. Why is configuration so important during engine-out operations?

## PROCEDURES AND MANEUVERS

1. Discuss the effects of banking the airplane toward the operative engine during single-engine flight.

2. What factors should be considered before shutting down an engine and feathering the propeller?

3. Explain why the takeoff and climb are considered to be the most critical phases of flight.

4. What procedure is used to regain airplane control if an engine failure occurs during flight below $V_{MC}$?

5. What indications does the pilot have that the airplane is approaching $V_{MC}$?

6. Is a successful engine-out go-around probable from a low altitude when the airspeed is below $V_{YSE}$?

7. Describe the use of the landing gear and wing flaps during an engine-out approach and landing.

8. In the event an engine failure occurs enroute, is the distance or time required to reach the alternate airport the most important consideration? Why?

9. If the right engine fails, which rudder will be required to counteract yaw?

10. Explain why rudder, rather than aileron, should be used to counteract the effects of asymmetrical thrust.

11. Describe, in sequence, the items on the single-engine emergency checklist that should be committed to memory.

12. Why is the throttle of the suspected inoperative engine retarded prior to beginning the feathering procedure?

13. Define accelerate-stop distance and explain why it is an important performance consideration.

14. When considering an engine failure, which is more valuable, airspeed in excess of $V_{YSE}$ or additional altitude? Why?

15. Does the shutdown of either engine affect the operation of the landing gear, flaps, hydraulic system, or electrical system?

16. If a positive engine-out rate of climb is not possible, how is the minimum rate of descent obtained?

17. What procedure should be followed if an engine develops low oil pressure, but the flight is close to the destination airport?

18. Is an engine shutdown recommended if low oil pressure, but normal temperature is observed?

19. Explain the steps necessary to secure the engine after complete engine shutdown.

20. Is it possible for the airplane to enter a single-engine stall before $V_{MC}$ is reached?

21. Why is it important to plan for an engine failure prior to initiating a takeoff?

## MULTI-ENGINE INSTRUMENT FLIGHT
### NORMAL PROCEDURES

1. Discuss instrument procedures pertaining to changes in power.

2. Describe the recommended trim technique during airspeed and/or attitude changes.

3. What are the primary considerations for a departure under instrument conditions?

4. What is the recommended holding pattern airspeed?

5. Why is preflight planning important for instrument approaches?

6. What are the main tasks a pilot is required to perform during an instrument approach (all engines operating)?

### INSTRUMENT PROCEDURES WITH ONE ENGINE INOPERATIVE

1. Describe the main pilot tasks that are required when one engine fails during instrument conditions.

2. What indications should the turn coordinator show during straight-and-level flight with one engine inoperative?

3. During engine-out flight, what approximate bank angle provides the best turning performance?

4. What is recommended concerning an engine-out missed approach in instrument conditions?

5. What type of approach should be requested for an engine-out, instrument approach?

6. What deviations from normal procedures, if any, are recommended for an engine-out instrument approach?

## MULTI-ENGINE ORAL QUESTIONS

1. What documents are required to be onboard the airplane during flight? Explain the significance of each.

2. Explain FAR 91.213 with regard to how it applies to flight with inoperative instruments or equipment.

3. Begin with the slowest V-speed shown on the airspeed indicator and describe each speed in order, including its significance.

4. Based upon the following data, determine the CG location.

   Pilot and front passenger. . .350 lbs.
   Center passengers. . . . . . 335 lbs.
   Fuel tanks . . . . . . . . . . . . . . Full
   Baggage. . . . . . . . . . . . . . . .75 lbs.

5. Use the weight and balance data from the previous question and assume that when an intermediate stop is made, the airplane has consumed 28 gallons of fuel and a 150-pound center seat passenger deplanes. How many inches will the center of gravity move and in which direction?

6. What grade and type of fuel and oil are specified for the airplane? How is the fuel checked to be certain the airplane has been serviced with the proper grade?

7. How is fuel contamination avoided during and after servicing?

8. Determine the amount of oxygen required for a flight at 15,000 feet for two hours with a total of three people onboard. How is the oxygen system checked and serviced?

9. Define the term *critical engine*. What determines the critical engine?

10. Define accelerate-stop distance and its significance.

11. Determine the accelerate-stop distance under the following conditions.

    Field pressure altitude . . . 2,500 ft.
    Temperature. . . . . . . . . . . . . . 52°F
    Headwind component . . . 10 m.p.h.
    Weight . . . . . . . . Maximum takeoff

12. Compute the takeoff distance over a 50-foot obstacle based on the following data.

    Field elevation. . . . . . . . . . 3,000 ft.
    Altimeter setting . . . . . . . . . . .30.20
    Temperature. . . . . . . . . . . . . . . 68°F
    Headwind component . . . 15 m.p.h.
    Weight . . . . . . . . Maximum takeoff

13. Using the data from the previous question, determine the takeoff distance with no obstacles.

14. What power setting will produce 65 percent rated power at 7,000 feet if the temperature is 34° F?

15. Based on the information from the previous question, determine the true airspeed and maximum range if the airplane is loaded to gross weight.

16. How does weight affect the stalling speed of the airplane?

17. Determine the stalling speed differential between the following configurations.

    Power . . . . . . . . . . . . . . . . . . . . . . Off
    Gear . . . . . . . . . . . . . . . . . Extended
    Flaps. . . . . . . . . . . . . . . . . Retracted
    Weight . . . . . . . . Maximum takeoff
    Bank angle . . . . . . . . . . . . . . . . 55°

    Power . . . . . . . . . . . . . . . . . . . . . . Off
    Gear . . . . . . . . . . . . . . . . . Extended
    Flaps. . . . . . . . . . . . . . . . . Extended
    Weight . . . . . . . . Maximum takeoff
    Bank angle . . . . . . . . . . . . . . . . 35°

18. Compute the average multi-engine rate of climb between the altitudes of 5,000 and 10,000 feet MSL under the listed conditions.

    Altimeter . . . . . . . . . . . . . . . . . . .30.17
    Temperature at 5,000 feet . . . 31°F
    Temperature at 10,000 feet . . . 0°F
    Weight . . . . . . . . Maximum takeoff
    Airspeed . . . . . . Best rate of climb

19. Based on the previous question, what indicated airspeed should be used to initially achieve the best rate of climb?

20. Given the following conditions, determine the average single-engine rate of climb between sea level and 2,000 feet MSL.

    Altimeter ................. 29.92
    Temperature at sea level .... 77°F
    Temperature at 2,000 feet ... 70°F
    Weight ........ Maximum takeoff

21. Explain how the best single-engine rate-of-climb and best single-engine angle-of-climb airspeeds change with an increase in altitude.

22. What is the single-engine service ceiling for the training airplane and what is its significance in relation to takeoffs and go-arounds?

23. Explain the relationship between density altitude and the single-engine service ceiling.

24. Given the following data, determine the landing distance required over a 50-foot obstacle.

    Field pressure altitude .. 1,500 ft.
    Temperature .......... 80°F
    Weight ..... Maximum landing
    Headwind ........ 15 m.p.h.

25. Determine the landing ground roll given the following conditions.

    Field elevation ....... 500 ft.
    Altimeter setting ...... 29.29
    Temperature ......... 65°F
    Weight ..... Maximum landing
    Headwind ............. 0

26. What is the correct takeoff and landing technique during operations on a runway that has an accumulation of snow or mud?

27. Explain the technique of using asymmetrical power during cross-wind taxi.

28. Explain the electrical system installed in the training airplane.

29. During single-engine operations, are there any restrictions and/or recommendations placed on the electrical system operation?

30. Discuss the hot starting procedure for the training airplane and explain how the pilot can determine when this procedure is necessary.

31. Explain the procedure for correcting an engine overheating problem.

32. Explain the correct and most accurate engine leaning procedures.

33. Explain and diagram the airplane's fuel system.

34. Discuss the proper procedure for fuel management for both twin-engine and single-engine operations.

35. Are there any restrictions placed on the airplane with regard to minimum fuel for operation?

36. What is the danger of operating an airplane with a leaking fuel strainer?

37. What is the procedure if an engine failure occurs below $V_{MC}$ on the takeoff ground run?

38. Under what circumstances may it be inadvisable to feather a propeller?

39. Once the propeller control is placed in the feathered position, approximately how many seconds are required for the propeller to feather?

40. List four methods of determining the inoperative engine.

41. Can the manifold pressure gauge and/or the tachometer indication be a reliable clue to which engine has failed?

42. Explain the propeller feathering procedures.

43. Is there any engine r.p.m. limitation on propeller feathering?

44. Explain the in-flight engine restart procedure if a propeller is feathered.

45. Explain why it is advisable to bank the airplane five degrees toward the operating engine during single-engine operations.

46. During single-engine operations, what is the slowest airspeed that is considered to be safe?

47. What gear/flap configurations and conditions were used to determine the published single-engine minimum control speed?

48. What is the proper recovery method if the pilot inadvertently allows the speed to dissipate to the single-engine minimum control speed during single-engine operations?

49. In the training airplane, is the greatest amount of drag created by the extension of the landing gear, extension of full flaps, or a windmilling propeller?

50. Explain the correct drag cleanup procedure for a go-around following a full flap approach to a landing.

51. How does landing gear extension affect the single-engine minimum control speed?

52. Is the landing gear electric, hydraulic, or a combination of the two?

53. How many seconds are required for the landing gear to retract fully? In what situation could this become critical?

54. Is it recommended for the pilot to make a definite effort to neutralize the rudder pressure prior to the landing gear retraction cycle?

55. What is the purpose of the landing gear safety switch and where is it located?

56. Which is the more critical situation—inability to extend or retract the landing gear normally?

57. Explain the landing procedure and configuration if the nosewheel will not extend and the two main wheels extend normally.

58. Explain the manual landing gear extension procedure.

59. What action should be taken in the event the propeller de-icing equipment fails on one prop?

60. If the airplane is autopilot equipped, is there any limitation placed on autopilot operation during single-engine flight?

61. What type of installation provides heated air to the cabin? Is there any limitation or restriction on this unit's operation?

62. Where is the alternate static source located and how is it put into operation?

# ANSWERS

## EXERCISE 1A—PROCEDURES AND MANEUVERS

1. True
2. False
3. 3
4. 2
5. False
6. absolute ceiling
7. False
8. D
9. A
10. B
11. E
12. C
13. K
14. I
15. L
16. J
17. G
18. H
19. F
20. E
21. B
22. A
23. C
24. D
25. False

26. False
27. 3
28. False
29. forced landing
30. True
31. fuel, baggage, passengers
32. 1
33. 4
34. 2
35. 1. Level off momentarily
    2. Open cowl flaps
    3. Enrich mixture
    4. Increase engine r.p.m.
    5. Use a higher climb speed
36. 1
37. 3
38. 2
39. 2
40. True
41. False
42. False
43. 1. Reduction in sound level
    2. Decreasing control response
    3. Aerodynamic buffeting

## EXERCISE 1B—GENERAL SYSTEMS

1. True
2. decrease
3. True
4. 2
5. engine-driven, electric boost
6. True
7. True
8. emergency single-engine
9. False
10. False
11. True
12. True
13. True
14. False
15. D
16. C

17. A
18. B
19. E
20. 4
21. False
22. True
23. gear warning horn
24. True
25. True
26. False
27. True
28. pneumatic, electric
29. True
30. gasoline combustion heaters, manifold heat exchangers

## EXERCISE 2A—WEIGHT AND BALANCE

1. D
2. G
3. H
4. C
5. E
6. A
7. F
8. B
9. 31,920
10. 100
11. True
12. 135
13. up
14. weight
15. 4
16. True
17. True
18. longer
19. 2
20. 5430, 43
21. True
22. 3
23. False
24. 32.4

## EXERCISE 2B—PERFORMANCE CHARTS

1. 4,200
2. 4
3. A
4. A, B
5. A, C
6. B
7. A, C
8. A
9. C
10. B
11. B
12. 2
13. 1
14. 2
15. 1
16. 31.45, 37.2, 202
17. 1
18. 3

## EXERCISE 3A—AERODYNAMICS

1. False
2. False
3. True
4. False
5. True
6. rate
7. 2
8. 3
9. 2
10. 1
11. C
12. E
13. G
14. B
15. D
16. F
17. A
18. 4

## EXERCISE 3B—PROCEDURES AND MANEUVERS

1. False
2. 3
3. inoperative
4. False
5. 4
6. rate
7. rudder
8. False
9. False
10. True
11. takeoff, climb
12. True
13. absolute
14. 4
15. time
16. 2
17. right
18. False
19. 1. Direction of yaw
    2. "Idle foot, idle engine" test
    3. The engine instruments
20. 1. Mixtures—rich
    2. Propeller controls—high r.p.m.
    3. Throttles—maximum power

## EXERCISE 4A—MULTI-ENGINE INSTRUMENT FLIGHT

1. True
2. fatigue
3. pilot actions
4. below landing minimums
5. cockpit management
6. missed approach

## EXERCISE 4B—INSTRUMENT PROCEDURE
## WITH ONE ENGINE INOPERATIVE

1. is not
2. gear, flaps
3. precision
4. should
5. $V_{YSE}$
6. True

# PREPARE WITH CONFIDENCE

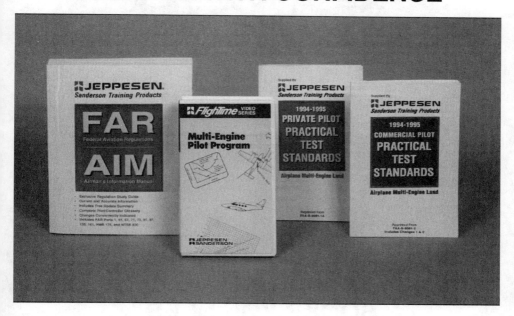

**FAR/AIM Manual** Comes complete with: Exclusive FAR study guide • FREE Update Summary • Complete Controller Glossary • FAR Parts 1, 61, 67, 71, 73, 91, 97, 135, 141, HMR 175 and NTSB 830 • Plus much, much more.
Item Number JS314107   $12.95

**FlighTime Video Series — Multi-Engine Program** Covers multi-engine aerodynamics, systems and performance, engine-out operations and instrumen flight through actual airborne and graphic sequences. Available with or without Jeppesen's Multi-Engine Manual.
Item Number JS200253 (VHS) W/Manual      $69.95
Item Number JS200294 (VHS) W/O Manual    $44.95

**Practical Test Standards** Jeppesen's Private Pilot and Commercial Pilot Multi-Engine FAA Practical Test Standards reprints are valuable training aids for instructors and students.
Private Pilot Multi-Engine Land PTS       Item Number JS315124   $3.70
Commercial Pilot Multi-Engine Land PTS    Item Number JS315631   $3.45

## Visit Your Jeppesen Dealer or Call 1-800-621-JEPP
Prices subject to change

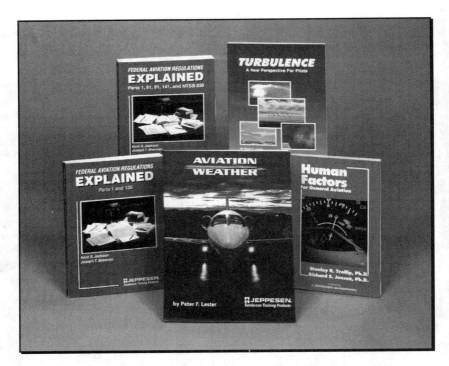

# BOOKS YOU NEED

**Aviation Weather** The most comprehensive aviation weather book ever published • Eloquently portrayed with over 400 pages and 300 illustrations • Each chapter includes learning objectives, key terms, FAA questions, insight readings, chapter summaries, chapter questions and references, and recommended readings to make learning effective
Item Number JS319007 $39.95

**FARs Explained (F.A.R.E.)** Jeppesen's F.A.R.E. has quickly become an industry standard. It helps answer the question, "I know what it says, but what does it mean?" These publications will save you time, money and frustration. Our standard FARs Explained includes FAR Parts 1, 61, 91, 141, and NTSB 830. And introducing our latest publication FARs Explained 135 includes FAR Parts 1 and 135. Each FARs Explained publication also includes: Plain language FARs • Easy to read and understand explanations to the FARs • Cross-references to other FARs to aid understanding • Actual case histories and FAA Chief Counsel Opinion excerpts. Order yours today!

FARs Explained       Item Number JS319012   $26.95
FARs Explained 135   Item Number JS319013   $26.95

**Turbulence/A New Perspective For Pilots** The most comprehensive, understandable book available on aviation turbulence today. Helps pilots recognize the conditions that cause turbulence, so the effects can be avoided or minimized. The book provides answers to questions such as: What is turbulence? • What does it look like? • How long does it last? • What causes it? • Where is it found? • What are its indicators? • What are the typical dimensions and intensities?
Item Number JS319006 $19.95

**Human Factors For General Aviation** Helps pilots analyze why accidents happen. This text covers: How to Identify Cockpit Design Problems • How Your Eyes and Ears Gather Information • What Factors Affect Your Decision Making • How To Use Cockpit Resources Effectively • Plus Much More.
Item Number JS319005 $34.95

## Visit Your Jeppesen Dealer or Call 1-800-621-JEPP
Prices subject to change

# JEPPESEN AIRWAY MANUAL SERVICES

**Airway Manual *Express*** Designed specifically for IFR students, CFIs and pilots who fly in small geographic areas, or fly outside their primary area of operation. Airway Manual *Express* is conveniently segmented into easy-to-use geographic regions. You purchase only the coverage(s) you need.

Complete new contents are issued every 56 days, eliminating the time required to organize revisions. A 28-day update is also available. The individual, all-in-one packets are availalbe by subscription and on a retail, single-issue basis from Jeppesen, your favorite pilot supply shop, flight school or FBO.

Airway Manual *Express* provides you with the same Enroute Low Altitude charts, Terminal charts (Approach charts, SIDs, STARs), Airport charts, Class B Airspace charts and Area charts found in our Standard Airway Manual coverages. Selected information pages are also included. State tabs, chart pockets and navigation plotter are sold separately.

| Area | Geographic Coverage | Single Issue | Annual Subscription (6 Issues) | Area | Geographic Coverage | Single Issue | Annual Subscription (6 Issues) |
|---|---|---|---|---|---|---|---|
| Southeast | GA, NC, SC | $18.95 | $84.75 | Alaska | AK | $16.95 | $74.75 |
| Mid-South | AL, KY, MS, TN | $18.95 | $84.75 | Central | CO, KS, MO, NE | $18.95 | $84.75 |
| Florida | FL | $16.95 | $74.75 | No. Central | IA, MN, WI | $18.95 | $84.75 |
| Mid-Atlantic | DE, DC, MD, VA, WV | $16.95 | $74.75 | Great Lakes | IL, WI | $18.95 | $84.75 |
| East | NJ, NY, PA | $18.95 | $84.75 | So. Central | AR, LA, OK | $18.95 | $84.75 |
| Northeast | CT, NH, ME, MA, RI, VT | $12.95 | $59.75 | Texas | TX | $19.95 | $93.25 |
| East Central | IN, OH | $16.95 | $74.75 | Michigan | MI | $12.95 | $59.75 |
| Southwest | AZ, CO, NM, NV, UT | $16.95 | $74.75 | Northwest | WA, OR, ID | $12.95 | $59.75 |
| California | CA | $18.95 | $84.75 | West Central | MT, ND, SD, WY | $16.95 | $74.75 |

**Airway Manual Service Binder** Functional. Durable. Protects and lasts. Jeppesen's vinyl binder offers economical protection and includes steel hinges and safety locks to secure the rings. This binder with 1 1/2″ rings is recommended for use with the Airway Manual *Express*.
Item Number AM621131   $10.95

**Airway Manual Accessories** Our complete line of accessories make your Airway Manual Service even more useful. These distinctive items are designed specifically to protect and help organize your flight information. You've got the best in navigation information. Our accessories help you get the most from it. • Contains: Chartabs (set of 3) • Approach Chart Protectors (set of 10) • NavLog/Flight Plan Forms (set of 50) • Multitabs (set of 13) • Pilot Notes (set of 25 lined).
Item Number AM626046   $12.95

**Professional Pilot Logbook** The book the pros use. Aviation's most popular professional logbook can handle 10 years of data. It includes simplified pilot and aircraft annual summaries. The quality construction matches the professional look of the Airway Manual binders. The gold signature strip allows you to personalize the cover with your own signature. (Size: 6 3/4″ × 11 1/4″)
Item Number JS506050   $19.95

**PV-5 IFR Enroute Plotter** It's almost like having an IFR instructor in the cockpit. Designed for use with all Jeppesen enroute charts, including area navigation (RNAV) enroute charts. Easy to use, it shows standard and non-standard holding pattern entries, as well as providing kilometer to nautical mile conversions. (Size: 3 3/16″ × 8 1/2″)
Item Number JS524409   $6.95

## Visit Your Jeppesen Dealer or Call 1-800-621-JEPP
Prices subject to change

# FlighTime Video Series
## Your Key to 60 Years of Aviation Experience

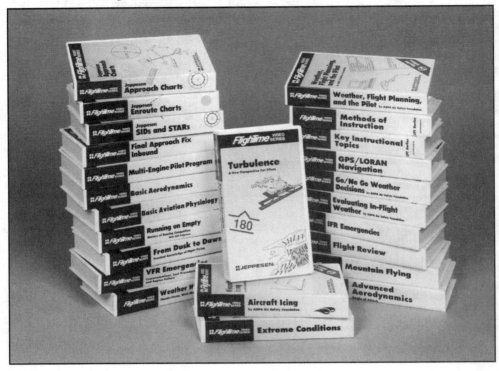

## INSTRUMENT FLYING

| Title | |
|---|---|
| Jeppesen Chart Series — 3 Videos | $97.95 |
| Approach Charts | 36.95 |
| Enroute Charts | 36.95 |
| SIDs and STARs | 29.95 |
| IFR Emergencies | 36.95 |
| Final Approach Fix Inbound | 36.95 |

## WEATHER TOPICS

| Title | |
|---|---|
| Weather Hazards | $36.95 |
| Extreme Conditions: Hot & Cold Weather | 36.95 |
| Aircraft Icing | 29.95 |
| Evaluating In-Flight Weather | 29.95 |
| Weather, Flight Planning & the Pilot | 29.95 |
| Go/No-Go Weather Decisions | 29.95 |
| Turbulence, A New Perspective | 29.95 |

## GENERAL SUBJECTS

| Title | |
|---|---|
| Mountain Flying | $29.95 |
| Basic Aerodynamics | 36.95 |
| Advanced Aerodynamics — Angle of Attack | 36.95 |
| Flight Review | 29.95 |
| VFR Emergencies | 36.95 |
| From Dusk to Dawn | 36.95 |
| Basic Aviation Physiology | 36.95 |
| GPS/Loran | 36.95 |

## SPECIAL TOPICS

| Title | |
|---|---|
| Multi-Engine Program | $44.95 |
| Running on Empty - (Soaring) | 29.95 |

## NEW CFI VIDEO SERIES

| Title | |
|---|---|
| Key Instructional Topics | $36.95 |
| Methods of Instruction | 36.95 |

## Visit Your Jeppesen Dealer or Call 1-800-621-JEPP
Prices subject to change